Trying to Get There:
Navigating Your Success

Trying to Get There:
Navigating Your Success

By Roderick A. Hardamon

White River Press
Amherst, Massachusetts

Trying to Get There: Navigating Your Success

© 2013 by Roderick A. Hardamon

First published 2013

ISBN: 978-1-935052-63-0
eBook ISBN: 978-1-887043-07-6

White River Press
PO Box 3561
Amherst, Massachusetts 01004
www.whiteriverpress.com

Library of Congress Cataloging-in-Publication Data

Hardamon, Roderick Akelo, 1976-
Trying to get there : navigating your success / Roderick Akelo Hardamon.
    pages cm
ISBN 978-1-935052-63-0 (pbk. : alk. paper)
1. Success in business. I. Title.
HF5386.H2497 2013
650.1—dc23
                          2012047712

Table of Contents

Author's Note

I want to break the mold!

Usually, when we read books on achieving goals or attaining success, they are told from the vantage point at the top of the hill. The stories, as helpful as they are, are told by a former CEO who has already taken over the corporate world. They are told by an athlete at the pinnacle of success. They are told from the vantage point of the entertainer who has already sold millions of albums.

While these stories are inspiring and motivational, I often wondered what the story would be like if it was told by someone who had not yet ascended to the mountain top, or someone who had not already earned the money, the fame and the accolades. What lessons could be garnered by a traveler still on the journey versus the person who has successfully completed it?

With that I offer this compilation of wisdom I have acquired on my own personal and professional journey. In addition to my own trials and tribulations, success and failures, triumphs and life lessons, I have added kernels of insight I have gathered from individuals I have encountered throughout my life.

To understand where this all comes from, I think it's important to understand **who I am** – and just as important, that you understand who **I am not**.

I am a reflection of who you are. I am a young, ambitious man trying to shape a better future for myself and my family.

I was raised in the inner city of Detroit, Michigan. I am the product of an educator with a Master's Degree and a factory worker forced to drop out of high school to earn a place in the harsh Jim Crow South.

I have several brothers and sisters, but I am the only offspring from the union of my mother and father.

I work in the world of high finance but help support members of my family who are on the opposite end of the economic spectrum.

I am the image of tailored professionalism during the week, with an extensive collection of colorful bow ties. However, on weekends, I am comfortable in sweat pants just as I am in a blazer and ascot.

I live in the corporate world, but I love old school hip-hop. I drive a Porsche… blasting Jay-Z from the speakers.

I raise my family in Detroit, Michigan but I travel to New York to earn my check.

I am a son and a father. I am a husband and a friend.

I am complex. I am the combination of a host of diverse experiences. I am more than you can see with the naked eye.

Simply put, I am **just like you**.

I am not the anointed CEO of a major company telling you how I made it. I am the guy on the journey telling you how I am trying to make it.

I am what you see when you look in the mirror. I am that mix of confidence and uncertainty that we all battle every day.

I have the desire that everyone has - to be accepted. We all have this desire that pulls against our longing to stand apart and rebel against the system.

I am not the corporate titan glorifying my life's accomplishments. I am the guy still trying to figure out the next ladder to climb, and what it will take to ultimately reach the top.

I am not at the climax of the story. I have only seen half of the movie.

I am, simply, Roderick A. Hardamon.

I am the son of parents who never implied there were limits to my life's possibilities. My parents encouraged me to explore everything life has to offer. They provided me with life lessons to achieve my loftiest goals, even if they could not imagine those goals themselves.

My mother instilled in me a passion for constantly learning and garnering more knowledge. My mother continued her education throughout most of her life. It was clear from her example that education was a lifelong journey.

My mother was a teacher whose touch was so powerful that people I run into 30 years after she taught them, speak highly of her as they refer to me as "Mrs. Hardamon's son." She was an administrator who treated every student and parent with the utmost dignity and respect. Through her actions, my mother showed them how to respect themselves.

From my father I understood the focus and determination it took to overcome life's many and difficult challenges. My father has a huge personality and is highly intelligent, but his education came mainly from surviving life's trials and tribulations. My father was born in Alabama during a time when African Americans were still not fully valued as citizens of this country.

He was born at a time when being black meant that you literally had to fight for your right to live and provide for your family. Though he never completed high school, I never once heard my father use his lack of education as an excuse for not being successful in this life. Though he appreciated the need for learning, he never dwelled on what he missed out on. Instead, he made sure that each of his children continued their education beyond high school.

From both of my parents I learned to value the complexity of life. The road of life is not always straight. It has twists and turns. The road is sometimes rugged and fraught with trials and obstacles. Yet these same challenges make the road interesting. It makes the journey more real and the rewards that much richer.

So join me as we begin our journey together...

Trying to Get There:
Navigating Your Success

SECTION I

GO GET IT!

CHAPTER ONE

Catching Your Wave

Imagine life as one great big ocean with a million different waves. Now focus on just one wave; one singular wave that fits the exact way you want to live, work, earn, learn, give and grow in your life. A wave that matches so closely to your own personal and professional journey that it may as well have been designed just for you.

It seems that way because it was designed for you. We each have a personal journey, a path only we can follow, a wave with our name on it. This book, this opportunity, is your chance to catch that wave and ride it for all its worth:

What's Holding You Back?

I welcome you to this journey. But before we begin traveling on this path together, there is one ground rule we must establish amongst ourselves first: for the rest of our travels together through these pages, we need to be open and receptive.

To that end I invite you to understand me a bit better. So, let me start by giving you some of the words that I hold most dear. Though these words and the others I will share throughout this book are from diverse individuals, each helps me frame a portion of who I am.

By sharing this message I am opening myself to you. I only ask that you open yourself to me:

"It must be borne in mind that the tragedy of life doesn't lie in not reaching your goal.
It lies in having no goal to reach.
It is not a calamity to die with dreams unfulfilled, but it is a calamity not to dream.
It is not a disgrace not to reach the stars, but it is a disgrace not to have any stars to reach.
Not failure, but low aim, is the real sin."
~ Benjamin E. Mays

What is the single greatest threat to our individual greatness?

This is a question I have asked myself and others for many years and the answer is always the same. Our greatest obstacle or impediment to success is not our individual circumstances or something external. It is something we all, struggle with every day and it comes from inside.

Our biggest threat, our largest obstacle, is simply **self-doubt**.

Self-doubt causes us to succumb to the pressures of the world. It allows us to become so paralyzed by the fear of failure that we accept our current status in life, no matter how unhappy we are, without even trying for something better.

If we are to have a chance at being great, of overcoming the toils of our current existence, we need large, grand dreams. We cannot be afraid of not achieving those dreams. The journey to achievement will provide lessons and learning that will be beneficial to our lives, regardless of whether we succeed or fail.

So, my first request on our journey: **suspend all doubt – do not think about what's not possible**. Open your mind to the endless possibilities of what you can achieve. Let's make sure our tragedy does not lie in having no goals. Let's not sentence ourselves to a routine life simply by failing to dream.

Microwaved World

In this digital age, we have become accustomed to instant gratification. We have grown increasingly conditioned to expect our rewards with little work or effort. When we are hungry, we can have a microwaved meal in minutes. When we want new music, iTunes delivers in seconds. Messages are sent virtually, instantly via text messaging. Although these have become common ways to satisfy the wants of our daily lives, the perception that everything in life will come just as quickly, poses a unique challenge as we seek to fulfill our needs.

I see this need for instant reward and acknowledgement in many of the professionals and students I meet, both young and old. They are all full of dreams and desires. They are filled with visions of corporate boardroom supremacy. They expect to be knighted as the next leader of the free world.

The energy they possess and exhibit is refreshing to those they encounter. The passion contained in their dreams is empowering. However, their lack of understanding of the road they must travel in order to achieve their goals is truly frightening. I know this for a fact as I am still learning this lesson myself.

This is a difficult lesson for most ambitious people to learn. We enter our chosen arena with the desire to excel, whether it be the world of high finance or the glamor of media and entertainment. We expect our genius to be recognized **on sight**. We expect those around us to see the aura of greatness exuding from our skin. If, by chance, those around us are too short-sighted to recognize our potential at first glance, surely after a year or so, we will be duly recognized. Once we have been "discovered," the distance between our current position and being the CEO is merely a stone's throw away.

Hard Work is Not an Option

Recently I was talking to a college senior about goals and expectations. As a part of the normal course of conversation I asked, "Where do you see yourself in five years?" The student's response epitomized the struggles of this generation of corporate professionals. After graduation, this young man planned to start his job at a large Wall Street firm. After two years, he expected to earn his MBA and then return to the work force making at least $500,000 per year.

Clearly this young individual had a warped perception of time, but the most disturbing issue to me was the lack of acknowledgement of the work and effort necessary to achieve even a fraction of his goals; it was all outcome, no input. There was a clear expectation that there was a standard formula for financial wealth – and apparently actual hard work was not part of that equation.

The focus on instant rewards obscures our vision from the truth. The reward is not some pot of gold, lofty title or endless power. The reward is the ability to continue your journey **on your own terms.**

Time is your friend and aide on this journey. It is not a deadline you need to beat, but a measurement of the depth of your experience that shapes your judgment and informs your decision making. Time allows you to prepare for the success you think you want. Sometimes, being intelligent, charismatic and ambitious is not enough. There is a benefit to experience.

The hardest thing for ambitious individuals to hear is: "You are not ready!" I know, because it's been hard every time that I've heard it. (Yes, it's been more than once!)

You Can't Win, Child!

As a nineteen-year-old sophomore at Morehouse College, I believed I had an enormous amount to contribute to my fellow students. I became very active in student government, serving as Deputy Chief of Staff as well as being very active in our student legislature.

As the academic year progressed, I became increasingly convinced that not only did I want to take a more active role in my student government, but I wanted to become student government president. Now, in and of itself, that particular goal was not unprecedented. What was different about *my* goal was that I wanted to win... as a sophomore.

Winning the position of Student Government Association (SGA) President as a junior was the norm and I had no desire to be normal. Nor did I want to wait a whole year to get into the mix and share my ideas on how the school should be run. For me, it was sophomore or broke.

Many of my peers tried to convince me that if I waited just one more year, I would have a very strong chance of winning. "Give yourself another year's worth of solid experience," they said encouragingly. "Make the right connections, vote on the right issues and build your platform first." Nope, not having it! Merely winning was not enough; winning extraordinarily was what I wanted to achieve – and the only real result that could satisfy me at the time.

Then again, I wasn't running simply to feed my competitive drive. I truly believed that I had something wonderful to offer to the college and the student body. I truly wanted to serve my fellow students. I just felt that they couldn't wait another 365 days to hear about it!

During the race, a friend of mine said something so profound that it has always stuck with me all these years. My man, G Ford, said, "Rod, you have potential, but timing is everything. You have to learn how to 'catch your wave.' Right now you are getting ahead of yourself and you will not win this."

Prophetic as they proved to be in later years, at the time, those words were like adding gasoline to a raging fire. Far from giving up, I became even *more* determined to win. After a very competitive and hard-fought race, I lost by a small margin. In hindsight, it was clear to me that I was simply not ready. In many ways, I was running against myself, my ego and my inexperience as much as I was running against the other candidates.

In life, we have to be cognizant of where we are in our journey of personal development, with a realistic assessment of our strengths, weaknesses, capabilities and limitations.

We all have to be critically honest with ourselves about what we are ready to take on. Just as important, however, we have to ask ourselves a few simple questions, like:

- **Is the timing right?**
- **Is the environment ready for my new success or idea?**
- **Is the company ready to promote me?**
- **Am I too ahead of the curve?**
- **Do my ambitions exceed my abilities?**

Grab Your Surfboard

This may all sound simple at first glance, but many of you are reading this right now thinking, "That's great, Rod, but… how do I know it's my time?"

Here are the three questions I would ask to help you find the answer:

1. **Am I prepared for the goal or success I want to achieve?**
2. **Have I made sure my environment is aware of my expectations and that I am ready? (In other words, have I told my story?)**
3. **Is this particular goal in the best interest for my overall goals in life?**

If you answered "No" to any of these questions, then you are not catching your wave!

So, what do you do if you're not ready? Trust me, it's not the end of the world. When I failed to win the SGA election in my sophomore year, yes, I was hurt and offended and took some time off to lick my wounds. But I didn't let my failure stop me!

I learned my lesson and moved on, and made the most out of my sophomore and junior years without letting this setback sideline me for too long. (I even served as chief of staff for the guy who beat me!) The fact was, once I sat back and looked at the contest objectively, I realized my friends were right. I decided to act on that "rightness" and put my efforts into moving just a little more forward every day.

It wasn't an overnight thing, it took a while. In many ways, I'm still learning, but that's the thing about waves: they don't stop coming – ever. Opportunity is out there for you, with every wave, with every phone call, handshake, job or promotion.

What struck me most about the experience of running for SGA President was how absolutely, 120 percent certain I was that this was my wave; the only wave for me. And yet, it wasn't. So I learned that riding someone else's wave is just as bad as not even grabbing your board!

Ride the Wave

I hit a point in my career about five years in where I needed to do something new. I had a great run working on some of the largest mergers and acquisitions in history. I lived in Asia, helping to advise large international conglomerates. I helped to complete very complex financial restructurings for some very troubled institutions. But despite all this success, I had the burning desire to learn something new.

I spent the first part of my career advising numerous companies on solutions to their problems. I wanted to take a more focused and in-depth look at one organization to determine how to help improve it. This was the first time I actually considered leaving Citigroup!

I had preliminary discussions with a few firms that were focused on strategy and development opportunities. As I had made up my mind to aggressively explore a career move, I was presented with the opportunity to help start a strategy team for a new business unit formed at Citigroup. It was a new business with a management team that had a reputation for being hard-nosed and aggressive.

Based on the recommendation of one of my mentors who had joined the senior management team, I strongly considered the opportunity. I asked myself those same three questions to ensure I had a good chance of catching my wave:

1. **Am I prepared for the goal or success I want to achieve?**
2. **Have I made sure my environment is aware of my expectations and that I am ready? (In other words, have I told my story?)**
3. **Is this particular goal in the best interest for my overall goals in life?**

Once I felt that I had sufficiently answered those questions, I decided to jump into the new role. Not only did the opportunity turn out to be a phenomenal learning experience, but it accelerated my career trajectory by several years. This one decision or opportunity is the key reason that I eventually became a Managing Director at one of the largest financial institutions in the world – all before the age of 32.

That's why I can state with such confidence that the key to achieving your phenomenal success is learning how to catch your wave. There are always waves in your life. Catching one does not guarantee you will catch the next, or that it will be the "right one" for you. Like snowflakes and opportunities, each wave is different from the one that came before it or the one to come after. You have to keep a mindful, dedicated eye on the progressions of your journey so that the wave you catch is the right one for you.

And most importantly… **__you cannot be afraid to get wet__**!

CHAPTER TWO

I Don't Play Craps!

Have you ever been so scared that you were afraid to act? Not just scared, but literally paralyzed by fear? I was riding my bike with my good friend Ahmar one summer growing up. As usual, we tended to venture off and explore new neighborhoods.

On one of our adventures we had ridden to one of the neighboring cities to see some friends of ours from school (which happened to be girls). We rode about five or six miles (which, at age 12 or 13 is pretty far from home) to a city that did not have any sidewalks.

Toward the end of the adventure I got caught in the street with a bus coming toward me. Forget "fight or flight," when I saw that giant bus barreling toward me, I instantly froze. I guess I thought there was nothing I could do to avoid the situation.

For what seemed like hours (but was merely a couple of seconds) I watched the bus rush toward me. Fortunately for me, Ahmar was still on the street, and was able to pull me back before the bus hit me. I was simply stuck, frozen – unable to move.

Getting Unstuck

I think we often get stuck on our journeys to success.

How many times have you been confronted with a wonderful new opportunity but, instead of going for it, you play it safe instead? Sometimes, we get so comfortable with our current lives, we are afraid to try something new.

Whether it's the opportunity to study abroad during college or take a job that, though it may not be viewed as attractive by most people, could teach us an entire new skill set, we decide to play it safe.

We don't ask for the new stretch assignment because we might fail. We don't raise our hands to move to a new country or new division because we are good at what we are doing now. It is simply easier to continue the status quo versus trying something new. Whatever else you call it, the fact is we are simply stuck.

Now, I am not suggesting that we should just randomly jump at every opportunity that pops up in front of us, regardless of how appropriate or inappropriate it may be for our future life plan. Every opportunity is not always a good opportunity, nor is every one necessarily bad. What we have to get out of it is the "habit" of discounting, outright, EVERY opportunity before weighing it fully. We have to take the time to evaluate each on its own merits and weigh its benefits for us.

The scariest part of this entire process is that we often make decisions about our future without fully understanding the opportunities in front of us.

We automatically assume that the new job is too hard or requires too many hours. We assume that we could never survive in a new country. We assume we would be starting over by moving to a new job. We assume, we assume, we assume...

But if we take the time to truly weigh the opportunity in front of us, we would see that there just may be a life-changing prospect right in front of our eyes.

But you'll never know until you try!

Buyer Beware

During my second year on Wall Street, I was faced with the decision to try to stay at Salomon Smith Barney or transfer to another firm. As I was part of a two-year analyst program, a job was not necessarily guaranteed for my third year. Instead, I had to apply for a Senior Analyst position. I had an intense first two years in New York working in the Mergers and Acquisitions group. After having pushed myself to the limit, working 100 hours a week (yes, I spent 60 percent of my life working!) I wanted my next experience to be just as challenging.

I had always wanted to live in another country, so naturally I thought this career crossroads was a prime opportunity to do just that. While most people chose to work in London for their third year rotation, I chose to move to Hong Kong.

I had studied a lot of philosophy and religion during my time at Morehouse College, so I had developed a certain appreciation for various cultures and customs. Correctly or not, I thought London would provide a relatively easy transition from New York; "easy" not being something I was particularly interested in at the time. Hong Kong, on the other hand, would be a real stretch. I would be forced to learn another language, be largely on my own and out of my comfort zone. I thought if I could survive in Hong Kong, I could do anything.

While I was making my final decision about whether to stay in New York or move to Hong Kong, several individuals attempted to persuade me from moving to Hong Kong. The first was when I happened to have drinks with one of my former senior colleagues at the firm. Let's call him "Allen," for the sake of argument.

Allen had recently left Salomon to pursue a senior position at a large private equity firm. Allen was a brilliant banker who had a reputation for being, shall we say, "overly direct."

Allen told me in no uncertain terms that if I moved to Hong Kong, I would be destroying my career as a banker. Period; end of story. If I wanted to truly learn how to do deals, he said, I needed to stay in New York. According to Allen, I was going to Hong Kong to "bury my career."

The second person that attempted to discourage me from moving was a senior banker from the Mergers and Acquisitions group. Let's call him "Neil." Neil had spent several years in Hong Kong and was attempting to give me some insight into the region.

In particular, Neil dwelled on the lack of diversity in the Hong Kong office (i.e. no black people) and the challenges of gaining acceptance with clients for all expatriates that moved there. He explained I might have a very tough transition if I decided to move to Hong Kong.

"Move at your own risk!" were his final words to me.

I think both Allen and Neil were attempting to be helpful in the advice they gave. They were giving me answers, direction and advice in direct relation to how they viewed the world. What's more, they were trying to protect me, to keep me on the safe "track" of what they'd seen work for both themselves and for other bankers. That track was very traditional, and I was anything but.

However, I had done my homework as well. In Allen's mind, being a banker meant purely being an investment banker; nothing else in the banking world mattered. What he did not understand at the time was that my perspective was very global. I wanted to understand how to be a global financial services executive. Simply doing deals was only a part of my learning curve.

Neil wanted to make sure I knew that no one could guarantee how I would be received by clients and colleagues. What Neil did not realize was that I was already used to being the minority. Neil had moved from New York, where he was one Caucasian male among many, to Hong Kong where he was the clear minority. So, for him, that was a new and potentially troubling experience.

Being a minority was not a new experience for me. I was used to having to adapt and collaborate with cultures that differed – often greatly – from my natural comfort zone. Actually, I think I was probably more prepared for Hong Kong than Neil was!

I ultimately decided to move to Hong Kong and it was one of the best decisions I ever made. It was there that I had a chance to experience my most significant personal and professional growth.

It wasn't all business for me. It was the first time I lived in an apartment completely alone. While I had wonderful friends who made my transition a lot easier (thanks Juliana and Karen!), I was truly on my own for the first time in my life. I learned a lot about who I was as a man and what I liked – and disliked – about myself.

I learned to be comfortable in my own silent thoughts, something that would have never happened in New York. I learned to take risks daily, like which path to take to work or what restaurant to eat at on a weeknight. Little things mattered and I noticed them more and more.

Professionally, I grew tremendously. Because we were a very lean staff, I actually spent 60 to 70 percent of my time in Seoul, South Korea covering large Korean conglomerates. I spent considerable time working with LG Electronics on a number of strategic initiatives and was a part of the team that advised LG Chemical on their demerger into LG Chemical Investment, LG Chemical and LG Household and Health Care.

While I am under no delusion that I was the best coverage officer on the planet, I gained significant insight into what it meant to be a trusted advisor and senior executive on large, lucrative and time-sensitive deals. My move to Hong Kong accelerated my development by several years and catapulted my confidence level by, literally, light years.

Unlike what Allen and Neil might have thought, I didn't necessarily "gamble" with my career, but I did take a substantial risk; one that paid off big time!

How to Weigh the Odds: *Questions You Must Ask Yourself Before Taking a Risk*

If you don't see the difference between gambling and risk-taking, then you're not paying close enough attention to the subtleties and distinctions between the two.

Gambling is playing a game of chance without the opportunity to apply skill, thought or aptitude. You pull an arm and the slot machine does the work for you. You buy a lottery ticket and cross your fingers and begin scratching. You can pick the slot machine or the store you bought the ticket from, but that's about as much "skill" as you can apply.

Risk-taking applies skill, aptitude, thought, decision making and counsel to an opportunity that may or may not pay off. So the next time an opportunity comes your way in the form of "taking a risk," take a step back and analyze it objectively by asking yourself these questions:

1. **What is the best possible outcome from this opportunity?** If this opportunity can accelerate you along your path of success, that's a positive, but first you have to understand how that will happen. Is it because you are learning new skills, or significantly expanding your network? Is it giving you responsibility faster than the traditional path or introducing you to a new one? Work to truly understand how you will benefit from the opportunity in more ways than simply, "More money." If you can't figure it out, maybe the opportunity isn't there to begin with.

2. **What is the worst thing that could happen if this does not turn out well?** You could get fired. But the funny thing is that, one day everyone gets fired. The best and most successful CEOs and entrepreneurs have been fired. Jamie Dimon, Sandy Weill and Steve Jobs **were all fired**. Everyone will be fired one day, but not everyone can say they took advantage of every opportunity to fulfill their dreams. Just because you are alive does not mean that you are truly living!

3. **How will I get back on the path to success if I get derailed?** Remember, there is a difference between taking a gamble and taking a risk. I always recommend going into a new situation with a back-up plan (reducing

your risk). Like my son who is a scout, I always try to be prepared. You never know how situations will turn out. Sometimes the best of intentions do not turn out right. You can't let one bump in the road derail your entire journey.

4. **How will this affect my family and other parts of my life?** Many of us act as though we live our lives in many separate worlds that do not affect each other. The work world is separate from the family world. The family is separate from the numerous causes we get involved in ... and none shall ever meet. However, the truth is that they all impact each other whether you know it or not. The choices you make about your career have a dramatic impact on your family and other aspects of your life, just like sometimes your family decisions impact your career. Good decisions are ones that weigh all of the impacts, and do not just ignore them.

When all is said and done, do you want to look back at your journey and say, "I always played it safe"? Or do you want to look back and proudly say, "I lived my journey to the fullest and embraced every success *and* challenge"?

Life is not a guarantee and it goes by very, very fast. If you measure your life merely by promotions, raises and gold watches, you are in for a very short, predictable and dull path. (And it still won't be without risk! Just ask anyone who invested their entire career in Circuit City, Borders or Hollywood Video.)

Hopefully, I will see you on the exciting path!

CHAPTER THREE

It's Not the C.R.E.A.M.

S torytellers of the future will likely recount the days of 2008 in a melodic composition of unyielding hope versus instability and despair. They will detail the hope emanating from the chants of "Yes We Can." They will describe the remarkable image of the new face of leadership in America. These visions of hope will be contrasted against the wave of hysteria that swept over the financial markets during this same period of instability.

History will chronicle how institutions that have existed for over a century, collapsed overnight. It will detail how Wall Street was remade over the course of a summer. The stories of fortunes lost will litter the pages of books and periodicals. They will tell stories of the automotive industry's tragic fall from grace and how their chieftains flew to Washington D.C. on private jets to beg Congress for help. The way the lives of everyday Americans were changed will be shocking. We will remember…where we were when…

Before I go on, I must take a moment to comment on the historic nature of the 2008 Presidential race. I will not profess to be the first person to jump on the Barack Obama band wagon. I initially had my doubts about his relative experience versus that of Hillary Clinton.

Over the course of her time as First Lady and Senator from New York, I studied Clinton's background and like most, became relatively convinced of her chances to become the first female President of the United States. As Obama began to emerge as a bona fide candidate, however, I wanted to make an informed decision based on his policies and views on improving the country.

As I proceeded to do my research (which included reading his positions and speeches), I began to be confronted by several individuals who expected me to automatically support Obama.

Now, my natural inclination in life is to always push back against individuals who aggressively attempt to influence my judgment. But as I did more research, I realized that Obama's views were relatively consistent with my own. Slowly, I began to truly open up to the idea of Barack Obama becoming President.

Now, I would love to say that it was my logic that ultimately led me to my choice of candidates in that historic election, but that would be a lie. In actuality it was my heart, or the little man inside my heart. I was looking at my son, Roderick Jr., or "RJ" as we call him, thinking about the conversations we would have 20 years from now.

I imagined RJ asking me about these historic times. I imagined RJ asking me how we survived the turmoil of the financial markets. Most importantly, I imagined RJ asking me about where I stood in the most important election of our time. When I thought about what my answer could be, I realized that there was only one option, one choice. From that moment on, Barack Obama had my support for President on the United States of America!

Now, back to the topic: It is often during the most unsettling of times in life when individuals believe they find themselves. They believe they discover what is important to them. I would argue that

21

people do not find who they are during these times but, instead, find out **who they are not**!

When times get tough, many people find that they are not mere mercenaries working for money or only seeking to accumulate wealth. They discover that they are not wanton power seekers climbing the ladder of success for self-gratification alone. Despite the famous words from the hip-hop group The Lox, people realize that it's not only about "Money, Power, Respect."

So if it's not about the C.R.E.A.M., what *is* it about?

If we are only trying to discover who we are when the world falls apart, it's already too late. Are we merely our ambitions and careers? Are we merely the size of our bank accounts or the sum of our material possessions? It's during these times that the pressure to succumb to outside influences becomes the greatest, making it even more critical to know "What are we in this for?"

Are we the hopes of our mothers and fathers? Our dreams of a better life for our future generations? Are we the collective lessons garnered from our spiritual foundations?

Now, not later, is the time to ask ourselves:

What Am I In It For?

I began my career as an investment banking analyst on Wall Street. I moved to New York to work in the high flying world of mergers and acquisitions. I spent my first three years working over 100 hours a week (the ultimate self-inflicted pain), trying to be the absolute best analyst at the firm.

I worked on transactions in the United States and Germany. I even lived in Hong Kong for a time. I worked on teams that advised large Korean conglomerates and executed some of the largest transactions ever announced in financial history. I made the rare jump for an African American from analyst directly to associate. I was on my way to becoming a high-powered investment banker.

Then something happened along the way to career nirvana; a little thing called... Life. I made the most important decision in my life and career: I married Kaili T. Davis.

Kaili comes from the same blue-collar environment of Detroit that reared me. We both came from modest beginnings where the focus was on family, not finance. Kaili was not the biggest fan of my maniacal work schedules and did not understand how we could have a successful marriage and family under those conditions.

Now, I would be a liar if I said I was not initially upset over my wife's disdain over my career path. But, as usual, my wife revealed a perspective on life that I often fail to see. Shortly after we were married, our son Roderick was born. Between being married and having a child, I realized that when it came down to it, being a wonderful husband and father was far more important to me than being a highly paid investment banker. With clarity, I realized that the 80- to 100-hour workweeks I'd devoted to my career could be much better spent creating a life. As a result, I decided to leave investment banking altogether. Although I left on my own terms, ultimately I left because I wanted more time for my family.

When they heard the news, many of my colleagues thought I was crazy. Why would I leave the prestige of M & A? What's more, why would I do it at the top of my game? After putting so much time, energy and personal sacrifice into my career?

The answer was simple: no one will ever remember, much less care, what deals I worked on and what headlines they made. But my son will remember whether or not I was a good father. My wife will remember whether she had me – or just money and gifts I earned while spending time away from her. This was the moment when I decided: family first, career second. I decided to make career decisions with a clear view of my family's happiness and of our future together. Every time I have been led by family, career success has followed.

Before you can truly know what you are in it for, you have to know how you are built. We are all like a house. A house is best when it is built with sturdy, durable materials. It must have a strong foundation and sit on solid ground. Like this house, we need to know how we are built to be our best.

Are You Standing on Quicksand?

The foundation for my "house" – my solid ground – is my spiritual foundation. You have to know the source of your power. Your power source is not what you have acquired; acquisitions are just ways to keep score of your financial progress. Rather, it is the place where you go to find comfort and solace in times of despair. It's where you seek out answers to the ultimate truths of life.

Whether you find your answers in the Holy Bible, the Koran or the Torah, you need a place to know where to find answers. When the storm comes, will you sink in the quicksand or will you stand strong because you are built on solid rock?

We all face many adversities and challenges throughout life. Some of these feel like annoying pebbles in our shoes. Still others are like a hill that is tough to climb. And then there are those other times that threaten to take everything from you. When you are faced with those life-altering situations, you need a strong foundation.

In June of 2011, I was on the verge of bringing home a very large deal. The team and I, in the Alternative Investment Services business I run, had been working on a significant piece of business for several months and the time had come to make our final presentation.

As this was a key decision point for the client, the team prepared tirelessly for days to ensure things would go perfectly... the best laid plans of mice and men. However, I awoke in the middle of the night the day before the meeting. I assumed I was anxious and needed to put in some extra preparation time. I then received a disturbing call from my wife. RJ was being rushed to the emergency room in Detroit. RJ was having a severe asthma attack. RJ has a history of asthma that is worsened during season changes. A short while later I received a call from my wife telling me they were going to admit RJ to the hospital. The third call said they were taking him to the ICU... to be intubated.

I hope you can imagine the pain and anxiety that washed over me. On the one hand, I had been preparing for a career-changing deal that my business sorely needed to win...and we needed to pro-duce. On the other hand, my namesake was potentially battling for his life. I did the only thing I could at that moment; I prayed for calm during the storm.

Then I made four phone calls:

1. To Delta airlines, to get the first flight possible to Detroit.
2. To my wife, to let her know I was there in spirit and would soon be there in person.
3. To members of my team, to tell them to bring it home without me.
4. To God...a prayer for the health of my son.

I spent the next 48 hours by my son's bedside. I wanted him to know that his parents were with him every step of the way. We received a host of love and support from family and friends. Their prayers helped keep us sane. After the most trying 48 hours of my life, RJ began to recover and the doctors removed the intubation tube from my son. Though he was not fully out of the woods yet, I knew the storm was passing.

Without having a foundation built on solid ground, I would have certainly drowned in the quicksand.

Forming An Inner Circle

The old adage states that, "Beside every good man is a good woman." While this is personally true for myself, the truth of this statement transcends well beyond my meager life.

We all have the best of intentions in life. We strive to be successful and honest. We strive to conquer the world. We put our faith in a higher power and do our best to live by the Golden Rule. But there are times when life seems overwhelming. There are times when the obstacles in front of us seem completely insurmountable, when our patience is tried, our faith is tested and our tempers are short. These moments are when we need to know there are people around ready and able to help us stay on track. I don't believe God ever intended us to walk through our journeys alone, and that one of life's greatest sins is denying others the opportunity to help strengthen their faith walk by helping you walk yours.

These people, be it mothers, fathers, wives, girlfriends, colleagues, neighbors or friends, are the foundation of your inner circle. It is this very specific, very personal cadre of souls that will help you fight when it seems that you have nothing left to give. They provide you with that word of encouragement on your darkest of days, and the encouragement to reach higher when you've hit rock bottom.

This is why the nature of your inner circle is so important. The individuals you surround yourself with are key components of your success in life. If the people you spend your time with have no dreams or ambitions, how can they relate to yours? What's more, how can they truly support you?

It's human nature to feel envy, particularly if you have little to show for yourself. If they are jealous and uncaring, how can they help you create a nurturing environment for you to excel? If they are not adding to the mix, they are taking away from it.

Sometimes we have to simply shake the haters off. For many of us, this is the hardest thing to do. We believe we should be loyal to our friends and family, often to a fault. This is particularly true if we grew up in a small town, or a sheltered environment or a close family. We are often loyal to those who give us nothing even at the expense of our own progress. What we often fail to see is that this only worsens the situation for all.

A line I heard once sums it up best: "I can't help the poor… if I am one of them." Whether individuals are "poor" in spirit, family life or financially, you have to transcend this state to set an example for others.

We have to make sure that our inner circle is comprised of the kind of people who create the foundation we need, not the one we want. They need to be honest, trustworthy, loyal, caring and spiritually grounded.

One of the most selfless examples of the people that make up my foundation is Miss Val. Miss Val has known me for five to ten years. She is one of the kindest, sweetest women I have ever encountered.

Miss Val had been working in the cafeteria at the office for several years. She had seen me grow from a young associate to

Managing Director. Whenever I saw Miss Val, she always had two things to say:

1. **How's Momma's son doing?**
2. **You make Momma proud.**

Our conversation never lasted more than two or three minutes. But in our brief exchange, she gave me the boost of energy I needed to let me know someone believed in me. She let me know she watched me fight the good fight and she told me she had been applauding me all the way. I just hope that in the few minutes we shared, Miss Val got a small measure of hope for what she could become as well.

Just like any circle, your inner circle is a never-ending loop of give and take. You support each other. In times of weakness, take what you can. In times of strength, give all you have. Miss Val is only one example of the many people who have supported my journey.

We should all be like Miss Val.

What's in You? *Candor, Loyalty, Empathy and Fortitude*

I am not a perfect man. Like most, in fact, I am very far from it. I make wrong choices every day. I seldom live up to the image I see for myself. I am no better than any of you. I try to live the best that I can every day that I can. I truly believe the only way to make it through life is to have a set of principles that build you up and that allow for growth, experimentation, and trial and error along the way.

These principles, like the bricks and mortar, beams and flooring of any house, are what you are made of. Build cheap, get cheap. Build strong, get strong. I am not trying to give a universal set of principles that will fit everyone. What I want to give you are the principles that guide my actions and my life, in the hope that they will lead you to discovering your own.

My four prime principles are basic and simple:

- **Candor**: When it matters, I will give you the honest truth as directly as I can.
- **Loyalty**: One of the most endearing human traits. I support those who have supported me and I expect the same in return.
- **Empathy**: To truly lead people, you have to understand and feel them.
- **Fortitude**: In the face of adversity, I don't wilt.

My principles are unquestionable and unyielding. That's what principles are; how you act in good times, in bad times, in strong times, in weak times and, most importantly, when no one is looking. They cannot be bought or bargained. Like the statement in the MasterCard commercial: My principles are priceless.

The most important element in my life is my family. So it would make sense that when it comes to my family my principles are unwavering... but they have been tested.

When my wife and I were married in 2001, she agreed to leave her job and life in Chicago to join me in New York. We began our "fairy tale" life together in a brownstone in Fort Greene, Brooklyn. We were all set to be a young vibrant couple enjoying everything the great city of New York had to offer. But life often has other plans. We soon discovered that we were expecting our son, "RJ."

Now, being from Detroit, neither one of us looked fondly upon the idea of raising a child in New York. We grew up with trees and backyards, not alternate side parking and community playgrounds.

29

So, after having been in Fort Greene less than a year, we packed up and moved to the Oranges in New Jersey.

We moved to a beautiful house in a good neighborhood at the end of a cul-de-sac. "Okay," we thought, "we finally got what we wanted!" During this time, Kaili decided that she wanted to pursue a career in education. Having received her Bachelor of Science in Mathematics from the University of Michigan, she desired to ensure that children grew up with a better appreciation and love for math. She enrolled in a Masters of Education program and began her journey.

So now we have two young people starting a new family with a beautiful baby boy, in a new house pursuing their careers. Sounds perfect, Right? Not quite, because something was missing: our family. We both grew up in tight-knit families in Detroit.

We were relatively isolated. Sure, we had family visit every now and then, but it really was "just us" for the majority of the time. I think most young couples underestimate the amount of effort and resources it takes to start a family. Having no family support meant limited babysitters when we wanted to go on an adult date. It was tough, to say the least.

In hindsight, it was also quite unfair on my part. I was still traveling to the New York office every day apart from other travels that I did, so it left my wife with very few options to develop her own social network in New Jersey. While my work life at the time was better than what I had in Investment Banking, I still worked a lot for the average person.

Beginning to feel the strain of being "alone" in New Jersey, we agreed to look at opportunities to move back to Detroit. In the spring of 2006, we began actively looking to move the family back home. I was in active dialogue with a leading financial institution in Michigan, while Kaili explored teaching roles in Detroit.

As fate would have it, Kaili secured a great opportunity for the summer, teaching math as part of a program for Wayne State University. Excited about the opportunity, we made arrangements for Kaili to move to Detroit for the summer and my Dad came to New Jersey to help me out with RJ. Not only did Kaili rock the summer, she ended up with multiple job offers to boot.

Now what do we do? Kaili had an opportunity to explore her dream in Detroit. My job was still in New Jersey. Do I try to play the "I make the money so the family should stay in New Jersey" card (I know some of you are thinking that) or do we find a way to make it work? This was actually the most pivotal point in our marriage for it would set the tone for the level of compromise we were **both** willing to make. Kaili made a sacrifice when she moved to New York. Was I willing to do any less?

We decided to give it a try with Kaili and RJ living with her parents in Detroit and me traveling there two weekends a month. (We could not afford much more at the time.) So for about six months, we experimented with the commuter lifestyle. During this time frame, I realized that Kaili really loved her job. She loved being closer to family. RJ loved being near his grandparents, uncles and cousins. If I was serious about putting family first, we had to find a way to make this thing work.

So in February 2007, we signed a lease for an apartment in the Detroit area. We firmly committed to living and raising our family in Detroit. As part of this plan, I approached the firm about setting up an arrangement to work remotely on Fridays so that I could be home in Detroit at least three days a week. Despite my initial hesitation about how people would react, the firm was actually very supportive of my decision. I have been commuting between Detroit and New York ever since.

Now, this may sound crazy to some and very untraditional to others, but there is one thing Kaili and I learned early: our marriage, our family, only has to work for *us*. It doesn't have to conform to anyone else's norms. It doesn't have to meet anyone else's expectations. It only has to be filled with love, respect, compromise... and it only has to work for us.

This was by no means easy. In fact, it was very challenging when we went through it. But because we put family first, because we stood on the principles of candor, loyalty, empathy and fortitude, we made it through.

Before you read any further, ask yourself these three basic questions about your own simple, basic and human principles:

1. **What grounds you?** It is very easy to get caught up in the accolades and accomplishments of life. It is very easy to ride the waves of euphoria of a great promotion or a great new job. But the thing is, those feelings eventually fade. There will be a new challenge to face that threatens to bring you down if you only rely upon the short-lived praise of others. The catch in life is never to get too wrapped up in the highs, nor too discouraged by the lows. They are both a part of your journey and make you who you are.

2. **Who is your foundation?** We all need a core foundation to keep us steady during the rocky times. While I have my family and my close friends, my steadiest foundation is my spiritual foundation. My belief in God keeps me calm during life's inevitable storms. We all need that anchor to help us stay in place, to hold our feet still when

the sands of time shift beneath us. Without that anchor, we will be blown about by any adversity we face.

3. **What are your principles?** We all need to understand what our core principles and values are. They define us and influence our actions. It doesn't matter as much what those values and principles are, but it is key that you understand them. They already exist within you and are guiding you in every step you take. So if they are there, it's better that you understand them. Once you understand what they are and if you like them, all is well and good. If you don't, now at least you know. And, as they say, knowing is half the battle!

So what am I in it for? I am in it to provide a financial foundation for my family. I am in it to provide an example for my children. I seek to progress so that my family and my community has an example of what a good man, good leader and a good human being look like.

Now that you know mine, it's time to find yours!!!

SECTION II

DO IT YOUR WAY

CHAPTER FOUR

Funky Fresh Dressed to Impress,
Or:
What is Your Personal Brand?

For what is a man, what has he got?
If not himself, then he has naught
To say the things he truly feels and not the words of one
who kneels
The record shows I took the blows and did it my way!
~ **Frank Sinatra,** *My Way*

Throughout our journey together, I hope to share more than a few insights that will aid you in your own great personal voyage to fulfillment and success, however it is you define it. But even if you remember nothing else from this book, you need to remember this: **Be an original; be you**.

The majority of the individuals we will encounter in life spend most of their time trying to figure out how to fit into the system. They try to imitate the behaviors and actions of everyone around them, assuming that if "the people worth imitating" succeeded in a certain, particular way, well, then they can too.

If they are surrounded by Ivy League graduates, they try to mimic their speech patterns, dress and actions. If they are surrounded by young, entrepreneurial rebel types, then that's who they'll imitate. If their boss likes hockey, guess who'll have rink-side seats next season?

Now I am not surprised that people mimic those around them. It seems to make so much sense to model yourself after those who have been successful. It seems perfectly reasonable to mold your own actions and interests based on a model that has already been proven to work.

What these misguided folks often fail to realize is that only by being a **<u>unique individual</u>** will you ever be noticed for your own personal contributions. Imitation might be the sincerest form of flattery, but it's the absolute worst path to success.

While personality can never substitute for talent, skill, and imagination, it's simply impossible to be yourself while trying to be someone else. We cannot be afraid to stand alone; to stand up when the crowd is sitting down. For when it's all said and done, we should be able to look the world in the eyes and proclaim: *I did it my way!*

Hello, World!

There is no mistaking that I am a black man. When I walked into Seven World Trade to begin my internship at Salomon Brothers, it was the only thing they knew for sure about me. They *hoped* I was intelligent and hardworking, but they knew for sure I was a young black man.

When I began my internship at Salomon Brothers it was clear to me that there were very few employees that looked like me, especially in the Mergers and Acquisitions group where I was first assigned. To say that diversity was a challenge is an understatement.

I knew from day one that I would *always* be noticed.

So, if I was going to always stand out, I wanted to stand out on my own terms. This is where I depart from many of my colleagues. Many people tell you that the way for diverse professionals, or any professionals for that matter, to succeed, is to keep your head down and work hard. They tell students and future professionals to "blend in" and not to be "overly" noticed. "You don't want too much attention," they'll tell you.

I contend that the fact that you are there at all is going to garner the attention, so use it. People will always be watching, either to see you succeed or fail. If people are always watching, what do you want them to see? Do you want them to see another average employee? Or do you want them to see an individual who can add something new and extra to the equation?

The first thing I wanted "the Watchers" to see was that I was intelligent and would outwork anyone and everyone. From the time I started as an intern, I worked as hard as humanly possible to get my job done.

I wanted it to be clear that not only did I have the analytical firepower to handle the rigors of working on Wall Street, but I also had the will and drive to be a "winner." I would take on assignments that I did not know how to do, then work non-stop for days, making sure I got them done anyway.

The first time I took on such an assignment was a few weeks into my internship. My senior associate noticed the effort I was putting in and asked me to do a net present value analysis involving tax benefits for a transaction. For those reading this right now, who don't have a clue what this means, don't worry; neither did I, at the time!

I did not even have a clue where to begin, but I knew that failure was not an option. So, I went to a different floor in the building and found a cubicle in an empty corner and called my cousin, Richard Hosey, who had previously interned at Goldman and received an MBA from Tulane University. Over the course of the next 45 minutes, Richard walked me through the mechanics of building my first discounted cash flow and Net Operating Loss (NOL) (tax loss) model.

I could have easily told my associate that I did not know how to do the analysis, and my associate would have gladly taken the time to walk me through it. But this was a critical opportunity for me to define what I could deliver, not just in this task but on every task.

I also knew it was a "test" to see how I would react: Would I need to be coached on every "i" to be dotted and every "t" to be crossed? Would I need to be walked by the hand through every project, deadline or deliverable?

This is an important point many people miss. Every new day, new assignment, or new interaction you have is in some way a test of who you are. Whether consciously or subconsciously, the evaluation process is always happening. The sooner you accept that process, the sooner you can start preparing yourself for it.

I wanted "the Watchers" out there to know that I was extremely resourceful; a self-starting problem solver who, above all else, **got the job done**.

The previous example set the very tone of my career.

From that point forward, I was going to be the "go to" guy for problems whether small, medium or large. I was going to be the one given the impossible tasks. I was going to be a solution provider, not an excuse maker. I was quickly and authoritatively developing a reputation as someone that delivers excellence.

I also started to become aware that in the corporate world, imagery was as important as performance. Although it would be nice to think that "the work could, and should, speak for itself," life just isn't that black and white. I started to understand that I could increase my visibility in the organization not just through my performance, but through my appearance as well. As with most things in life, this was a lesson I stumbled upon by accident.

The Bow Tie Experiment

The normal attire on Wall Street consists of tailored blue and grey suits, white or blue shirts and long ties; overall, corporate attire is traditional and conservative. Now, having gone to Morehouse, the bow tie was a fixture in my professional wardrobe. I decided to wear bow ties at least once a week as a way of expressing myself.

At first, my bow ties garnered little attention. However, slowly, I began to notice that many people began to make jokes about my ties. This came to a head at the end of my first year at the firm, when all of the second year analysts in Mergers and Acquisitions decided to spoof my attire by wearing a variety of silly bow ties; the sillier, the better. The entire group got a good laugh that day.

Though it was all done in good fun, I was faced with a choice. If I followed the traditional wisdom, I would have surmised that I was drawing too much attention to myself and stopped wearing my bow ties. Fortunately, I have never been conventional!

Instead, I redoubled my efforts and started wearing bow ties *twice* a week. When people made more remarks, I began wearing them three times a week, then four days, then every single day. I decided that the bow tie was going to be one of my calling cards. It would be the visual representation of my own unique and personal brand. It would convey that I was serious and refined, yet not afraid to stand apart from the crowd. Today, it has become such a part of my personal brand that people question when I *don't* wear a bow tie.

Now *that's* coming full circle!!!

Appearance + Performance = Perception

From that time forward I became intensely focused on my overall external perception; on my image. When I moved to Hong Kong, I was highly concerned about how clients and colleagues would perceive a young African American professional. Would I look too young? Would my age mark me as inexperienced? Would my external image match my developing dynamic professional reputation?

So, to aid the transition I did the following two things:

1. **I upgraded my wardrobe to look more professional**
2. **I grew a beard**

Now, most would think that a beard would be the last acceptable thing at a Wall Street firm. But I surmised that the facial hair added a few years to my age, making it easier for my new clients and colleagues to receive the information I provided.

Now, don't get me wrong. I will be the very first to admit that, without substance, **<u>appearance is irrelevant</u>**. Playing dress up for dress up's sake was never my style, nor my recommendation. But the combination of substance plus performance along with a well-crafted image is powerful, powerful stuff. Because my facial hair experiment helped me succeed in Asia, I have worn a goatee or beard ever since.

The combination of my professionalism, demeanor and visual image helped me to create the aura of a professional with experience far greater than I had legitimately achieved. My theory was validated years later when I was leading a European acquisition for the firm. A few of the senior team leaders were sitting around the table over dinner and the topic turned to age and experience.

Usually, when those topics come up, I tend to disengage from the conversation. As everyone went around the table talking about their 15 or 20 years in the business, everyone naturally assumed that I had similar time invested. When I revealed that I had only been working for seven years at that point, the group was floored. One person literally almost fell out of his chair.

Mission accomplished!

Define Your Brand

I have spent years crafting the image I want people to perceive. Rather than just a cosmetic one, my image has been developed by – and crafted over – years of excellent performance, quality judgment, and tested leadership. It is exhibited through my tailored wardrobe and colorful bow ties. Most importantly, my brand represents who Roderick Hardamon is at the core.

My brand is not a mask I put on when I walk into the office. It represents who I am seven days a week; just a more professional version. It reflects my focus on excellence and achievement. It reflects my love for fine clothing. All in all, it reflects my willingness to stand alone and be visible.

Now the question for you:

What Does Your Brand Say About You?

I once heard someone answer this question with, "I don't know what my brand is."

Or, even scarier, "I don't have a brand."

The fact is, you do have a brand. Consciously or subconsciously, what you choose to do, defines your brand just as surely as what you choose *not* to do – or even ignore – about your brand. It's a lot like the statement I made earlier: people are going to be looking at you anyway, so make sure they're looking at the image you want to convey, not the one they paint for you.

Whether you realize it or not, how you speak, dress, interact, laugh, walk, argue, and even play tells the people around you **about you**. Everything we do – or don't do – sends a message, telling people whether we are warm and personable or distant and reserved. It tells people whether we care about the details as seen through the attention we pay to our appearance. Others can tell whether we are effective communicators by the way we both listen and speak.

We are constantly sending messages about our brands. If you have not spent any time thinking about your personal brand, then it is probably (almost assuredly) *not* telling the story you want!

So, now that you are thoroughly convinced (or frightened) about the need to at least understand what your brand is: there are some basic questions you need to ask yourself in order to begin the journey of crafting the right image that works for you.

While the following questions are not an exhaustive list, I think that they will get you started with figuring out the right questions to then ask yourself. And if you come up with your own remarkable questions, share them! Now, for the questions:

1. **What does my personality (demeanor) communicate about my interest in dealing with people?** Sometimes we take the basics of how we deal with people for granted. We don't always recognize the tone or language we use when we speak to others, or the overall energy we give off. Because we overlook these basic things, we often fail to appreciate the impact they have on how others deal with us.

   If you are reserved, then understand others may be less willing to open up to you because you are not open to them. If you are overly aggressive, understand some may be intimidated by interactions with you. If you fill a room with your personality, others may be reluctant to speak up for the fear of being overshadowed.

   No one personality is inherently good or bad, we just need to understand how our own impacts the waters we swim in. Being reserved, for instance, doesn't necessarily mean that you're not interested in the lives of others, only that you're not as naturally outgoing and effusive as you might like to be. Start with small steps. Begin by engaging a new person each week. Get to know who they are as a person. Do they have a family? How do they spend their free time? Over time it will feel more natural until it ultimately becomes second nature.

   If you're a standout personality used to taking center stage, think of how your "audience" might feel and put yourself in their shoes. Consider letting others take center stage without feeling threatened that you're no longer in the limelight. True leaders know when to take a back seat!

2. **What does my attire say about me - professional and/ or casual?** Let's get right to the point: your outward appearance matters! When you walk into any room, the

first thing people know about you is what they see and, whether we like it or not, impressions are being formed based on that initial image.

And those first impressions are very, very hard to erase!

So, if that is the case, why not make the first impression as positive as possible? One way to improve the probability of making a great first impression is to be appropriately attired. Most of us would find it awkward to show up to play basketball without gym shoes and a basketball or to play tennis without a racket and shorts.

Accordingly, we should feel equally as awkward to show up to a professional workplace without the appropriate equipment and/or "uniform." The time we spend picking out our attire says something about how important we are to ourselves. If you are not important enough to invest your own time in, why should anyone else invest time in you?

3. **What does my conversation imply about my personal or professional interests?** Talking is easy, but conversation is a (learned) skill. Too many of us talk but don't listen, or only pretend to listen. It is truly important to have strong conversational skills that are equal parts speaking with confidence and listening with empathy.

   Let's take the speaking part first. What you say is just as important as how you look and even as important as how you perform. Words matter, particularly to those who are investing time, money, and resources in hiring or promoting you. How you talk to people lets them know not only what you are interested in – a good time, career growth, being a team player, etc. – but also that you are interested in them.

Now, for the harder part: listening. Merely being silent while someone else is speaking is not enough. Listening is a trait that goes a long way in fostering communication between you and whoever you're talking to: employee or employer, friend or stranger, family or acquaintance, client or competitor.

It's easy to think that we can talk our way into a job or out of a problem but sometimes listening helps get the job done sooner and avoids the problem altogether! And remember, talking too much will always get you in *more trouble* than listening too much.

4. **What does the way I spend my time communicate about what I hold most dear?** Now, more than ever, the work-life balance is blending into a daily concoction that can often look blurred. Where does our work end and our life begin? I can tell you at various times in my life, work was my life. Now it is part of my lifestyle, but even that has ties back to work and how my own personal brand is perceived.

What are your interests? What are your hobbies? What movies do you like? What's your favorite sport? All these factors tell others about you and your personal brand. They can also be revealing if you've never really chosen to ask yourself: How do I spend my time?

Since my family is my lifeblood, they represent much of my free time – and that's what's so great about it!

Since my appearance is important to me, I spend a lot of my time on health, grooming, and physical concerns: exercising, eating right, staying current with styles and trends.

Since work is important to me, I spend other segments of my free time improving my professional self, through reading a self-help book on the way to work or networking with other professionals.

Since giving back is important to me, I spend my time supporting organizations with focuses ranging from leadership development, to education, to the performing arts.

5. **What does my smile say about me?** You may think that something as simple as a smile has no bearing on your personal brand, but when it comes to first impressions and personal brand, body language is often as critical as verbal language.

   Your smile, or lack thereof, can tell people a lot about you:

   - **Are you happy to be there?**
   - **Are you interested in the person you're smiling at?**
   - **Are you alert, active and engaged?**
   - **Or are you bored, distracted and uninterested?**
   - **Is it a forced smile, indicating you'd rather be somewhere else?**
   - **Does your smile reach your eyes (i.e. is it authentic)?**
   - **Is your smile instant/immediate?**

   All of these questions and more, believe it or not, can be answered simply based on the strength, or weakness, of your smile. Few things are less sincere than a forced smile, so work on being authentically and enthusiastically engaged whenever you meet someone new. Find something to be interested about, to learn or share, to understand or explain.

6. **What does my willingness to stand out say about my ability to take risks?** When you are willing to stand out in a crowd of very similar people, it definitely sends a message that says: "I am an individual." It also says that, according to popular conventions, you're not afraid to take a risk.

   Again, substance over form. No one is suggesting you wear a mohawk or a spiked dog collar around your neck to show what a risk-taker you are, but as part of your overall brand, your appearance does speak volumes.

7. **What does my willingness to stand alone say about my self-confidence?** Regardless of the field you're in, or aspire to be in, this much I can tell you: confidence is in short supply. This is an almost universal truth experienced by nearly every CEO, VP, coach or consultant I've ever worked with.

   Now, you may be shaking your head but consider this: overconfidence is acutely in abundance. I never said it wasn't. But as most of us know, overconfidence is typically an overcompensation for insecurity.

   What I'm talking about is true self-confidence, the assurance to believe in yourself enough to stand out from the crowd, to stand on your own two feet and travel in your own unique direction, even if everyone else is heading the other way.

   There are a lot of unspoken factors when it comes to personal branding. You can dress a certain way, speak a certain way, and smile a certain way, but if any of these comes off as mere "armor" or a "costume," folks will notice. People want to work with, work for, or hire, other people who are confident, poised and self-assured. Confidence is something, you can't fake, and it's a critical factor of your personal brand that comes from the inside out.

To Stand or Not to Stand

Now, some of you are no doubt asking yourselves right about now, "Are there any downsides to standing out?" Well, yes and no. The answer actually has a lot to do with your personality and how you react to attention.

This much I do know: standing out from the crowd keeps the spotlight on you. It highlights your successes, your triumphs, your achievements and also your failures. The more people watch you, the more you get noticed, and get this – the more people will expect to watch and notice you. When the spotlight is on you, your successes seem grander and, more significant, but so do the inevitable challenges you face.

Frankly, I wouldn't have it any other way. I want the spotlight shining on me because I am always willing to bet on my ability to succeed, to win, adapt, achieve, and overcome. I am willing to put in the effort, preparation and energy to ensure that when people see me, when I feel that spotlight's glow I will be representing myself to the utmost of my abilities.

If I fail at something, it will not be because of a lack of effort or dedication. I am always willing to risk failure because the failures will teach you the lessons that allow you to have the significant triumphs. As long as I can look myself in the mirror and say that I did my best, I can walk with my head held high, no matter how bright the spotlight might shine.

I refuse to be guilty of aiming too low, at not dreaming big enough. We should all strive for the stars and get sore daily from grasping too far beyond our reach.

I know it feels safer out of the spotlight, safer to stand on the sidelines. I know it seems more comfortable there, more secure. It's easier to hide our failures from others when fewer people are watching. But here is the catch: while you can hide from everyone else you can never hide from yourself. You will always know that you did not live up to your potential. You will always know that when the lights came on, you had to run and hide. You will always know that you're just merely biding time...almost sleepwalking through life. And while the people in your life will change, the one constant will be the person in the mirror.

If what you want is success – then you have to get comfortable stepping out into the spotlight. You have to get comfortable being just a little bit uncomfortable. After all, if there are no ups and downs in your life, then it means you've flatlined, personally and professionally: or simply put you are boring yourself to death!

Finally, here is one more reason to stay out of the shadows: if the spotlight is constantly on you, it's hard for "the Watchers" to see everyone else.

CHAPTER FIVE

Swagger: Do You Have It In You?

S wagger has been the most overused word in popular culture over the last several years. While used by everyone from sportscasters to hip-hop artists, it is probably one of the most difficult words to define. Synonyms range from "strut" to "bluster," "arrogance" to "conceit," but generally swagger seems to be a state of mind; an attitude, an energy, an air that one carries about himself.

Although difficult to put into words, we all know swagger when we see it. We use it to describe entertainers we idolize for their self-confidence and talent: Denzel Washington, Jay-Z, George Clooney. We use it to describe leaders who capture our attention with their mere presence: Barack Obama, Bill Clinton, Colin Powell. We use it to describe our athletes who project an inner confidence that we admire: Michael Jordan, LeBron James, Roger Federer. We use it all the time... but do we really know what it is?

Swagger is the combination of numerous qualities that combine to form a uniqueness that stands out in a crowded room. Being merely confident or well-dressed is not enough. Having presence or being well-groomed is also insufficient. Being articulate and poised is only part of it. Being intellectual and sartorial is not enough. All of these qualities in and of themselves are a benefit to have, but none alone give you swagger.

So that begs the question: what *is* it? Swagger is that undeniable force that is created when all of these qualities are present in a perfect balance for a particular individual. That's really the key component of swagger: individuality.

What adds to one person's swagger may actually detract from another's swagger. A key aspect of Michael Jordan's swagger is his arrogance toward the competition. By contrast, it's Barack Obama's ability to be strong yet cooperative with rivals that helps define *his* personal swagger. Kanye West takes self-confidence off the charts to define his swagger, while Jay-Z prefers to speak softly and let his copious talent, business acumen, and humanitarian efforts speak for his swagger.

That's what makes swagger so interesting and, for some, so frustrating: it's never the same combination twice. Every person that has that something special has one of these qualities slightly out of balance. Though they may be poised, they also exude a presence that energizes a room. Though self-confident, they have a way with words that tickles the ear and serves to soften their bluster. Though sartorial, they have an ability to draw in the common man.

Audio Tuning

In the end, I think the most visual description of what swagger is comes from a good friend of mine, who described it like a graphic equalizer on a stereo system. On the simplest of equalizers you have your bass, treble, fader, etc. Depending on the type of music you listen to, you may have grown accustomed to bass-heavy tracks and thus tend to let the bass dominate the music. Or you may have grown up listening to rock and prefer to have the treble dominate the track.

Now, for your everyday listening, each of these settings is fine, even desirable. Then one day you hear the same song you have listened to for years on a finely tuned system. The bass is in its proper balance and the treble is not too understated. At first listen, the music sounds different, even new, yet familiar all at once. Then it kicks in that you not only know this track, but it's your favorite song.

You don't know exactly what's different about this particular listening experience versus all of the others, but you do know that it just sounds right. You know that, this time, maybe for the first time, it's special. You know it's the way the music was meant to be heard. You know, because it just feels right. That's what swagger is: the feeling that things are in balance; the confidence, poise, appearance, the right energy.

Mr. Cool

Now, I don't know when I first used the word swagger, but I know the first time I knew someone who had it. In 1997, I was a junior at Morehouse College. Morehouse has a program within their business department that affords juniors and seniors the opportunity to travel abroad during spring break. Dubbed the "International Spring Tour," the trip is designed to expose students to international business culture and practices to provide insider insight and perspective. A heavily sought after experience, I was privileged to attend on the trip that traveled to Rio de Janeiro and Sao Paolo, Brazil, and Johannesburg and Cape Town, South Africa.

Normally, the trip consists only of students and faculty for the 10-day excursion. When we landed in Africa, most of us were in awe. We were eager to experience being on the continent and touching a piece of our heritage that seemed unattainable. When we landed in "JoBurg," we had an unexpected addition to the group. We were joined by two Morehouse Alums who decided to join in on our experience. While the addition of the alums added a special dynamic to the occasion, there was one individual who stood out: Mr. Shaka Rasheed.

Shaka was a popular alum who had a distinguished reputation at the college. As former SGA president and current Wall Street professional, Shaka was perceived to have achieved a certain level of success, having only graduated a few years earlier. Though talked about greatly, most of us had never actually met Shaka before. When Shaka showed up in Johannesburg, he was the epitome of cool.

The mere fact that he could leave work to come to meet us in Africa surprised us. We had never imagined or contemplated that an alum, let alone a recent graduate, would join us on our adventure. To top off our shock, Shaka stepped off the plane in a sweater and an ascot... and pulled off the ensemble without missing a beat. Shaka was down to earth and humble, yet commanded a level of respect by his mere presence. He was dapper and supremely confident, yet he was completely humbled to be there with us. Not only were we (or at least me) in awe of Africa, we were in awe of Mr. Rasheed.

Over the years, I have gotten to know Shaka well. While I have lost some of the youthful luster that inspired our jaw-dropping introduction, Shaka has lost none of the swagger from our first encounter. Since our first meeting that time he has gone on to earn an MBA from Harvard Business School and later went on to have a very successful career on Wall Street. He has done this in a very staid and dignified climate and never lost his swagger.

Swagger Like Us

Now, every person you ask will likely try to frame this special composition in a different way. So I will give you my perspective. However, instead of trying to come up with a definition, let's focus on some of the special qualities that we recognize in various individuals whom you're sure to identify immediately:

- **Self-Confidence:** Michael Jordan, LeBron James, Lady Gaga, Kanye West, Beyoncé
- **Intellectual Integrity:** W.E.B. DuBois, Cornell West, Na'im Akbar
- **Sartorial Splendor:** André "3000," Frank Sinatra, Jane Kennedy
- **Elocutionary Elegance:** Martin Luther King, Jr., Malcolm X, Bill Clinton
- **Presence:** Barack Obama, Kofi Annan, Morgan Freeman, John F. Kennedy

There is one unifying aspect that connects each of these unique individuals. When you are in the company of an individual that has that something extra, you are quite aware of it. You can feel the energy they exude. Almost everyone who's ever met Bill Clinton can tell you that his presence literally fills the room; it changes the very chemistry of the atmosphere into which he is placed.

Swagger is as much about the characteristics that an individual embodies as it is about the energy that resonates from their persona. There are many individuals in the world that have wonderful qualities. Many are highly intelligent and possess a level of self-confidence and certainty. Others are well-dressed and articulate. However, the problem many of them have is that they are afraid – or unable – to let these qualities be visible to others.

When they are around other people they become "shrinking violets," sucking energy from the room rather than adding to it. They do not allow their natural light to shine and warm those around them and it is this inability to shine in the dark that prevents them from having swagger.

When I talk to people about swagger, there are always two stages to their reaction: The first stage is the instant acknowledgment and recognition of what they believe swagger really is. They either believe that they have "It" or they have personally experienced it in someone else. However, the second stage is the more interesting of the two. When these people are pressed to articulate what they believe swagger comprises, there is usually a long pause followed by the most descriptive phrase in the English language: "Well, you know." After the first attempt, they usually begin to describe a situation where swagger was absent.

Here's a good example of what I mean: I was having dinner with a long-time friend of mine who is a pastor as well as a philosophical scholar, and as we began to talk about what swagger is, he immediately began to detail a challenge he was facing with one of his ministers. To frame the situation, my friend is a very active individual with a big personality. In addition to being a dedicated pastor, he is a frequent public speaker, community activist, graduate student pursuing a doctorate in Philosophy. Now *that's* swagger!!!

Given his taxing schedule, my friend wanted to encourage a new member of his staff to take a more active role in the Church. He encouraged this individual to take ownership of programs focused on the Church's community outreach initiatives. However, the minister needed significant guidance and direction, which were additional burdens on my friend's time. The inability to take initiative, or lack thereof, concerned my friend deeply. But what really was concerning him was that there seemed to be something missing. It seemed this minister was missing the awe factor. It was apparent whenever he was dealing with the congregation and apparent in his dealings with my friend, the Pastor. The minister did not have enough presence to capture a roomful of people. He was simply missing that special air of authority required to inspire a congregation.

This was just one of the many stories I heard as I tried to understand what people thought it took to have swagger. In each case, the individuals that I talked to ended up not defining what swagger was, but highlighting what it was not, or even when it was missing. And therein lies the rub: we may not know what swagger is, but we definitely know when it's not present.

This is the critical message for each of us on this leg of our journey. Everyone may not know when you have swagger…but they damn sure know when it's missing.

Now, before we conclude the topic of swagger altogether, here are five critical questions for you to answer:

1. **What makes up your swagger?** List a few of the elements that make up your own personal swagger. Be specific, and take your time to come up with traits that are unique to you, and that you also best exemplify.

2. **What one word or phrase would you use to describe your own brand of swagger?** Once you've come up with the various definitions and traits of your own personal swagger, boil them all down to come up with one word that best describes how you swag.

3. **Is your swagger true and honest or are you just faking it?** While all must come to find their swagger in a new and unique way to them, one thing that defines all types of swagger is this: authenticity. It must be real and, you must feel it deep down, authentically, in order to own it.

4. **Are you comfortable with your level of swagger?** That being said, how comfortable are you in your swagger?

5. **Most importantly, does your swagger portray the type of person that you want to be?** Kanye West, Madonna, Lady Gaga – these folks are all more than comfortable being supremely confident, even arrogant, as part of their swagger. Not everyone can be so bold, nor should they be. If you're not comfortable with your swagger, then it's not your swagger, it's someone else's.

When you boil it all down, swagger really comes from finding your true self. It's about embracing those unique and special qualities that you possess. It means not being afraid to let your personality shine. It means not being afraid to be the intellectual you truly are. It means not shying away from that great opportunity because you know you want to take more risks. It simply means being you in all your strengths *and* faults.

We cannot be afraid to stand up and embrace our areas of development. The trick is (and I learned it in a leadership training course myself) that your best attributes oftentimes can be your most significant inhibitors to your success. In not being able to own your faults, how can you ever truly own your greatness?

CHAPTER SIX

King Kong Ain't Got Nothin' On Me

I have heard the old maxim, "work hard and keep your head down," many times throughout my life. I imagine that whenever these words are spoken, they are suggested with the best of intent. They are a call for substance over form. They are words of encouragement to the young to actually get work done, versus just talking about doing it. It's a call to engage in the business of doing good work.

This is important for all of us to learn: **Nothing trumps substance**. There is no better builder for your brand than consistently delivering at a high level. It helps to steer people's perceptions toward quality and excellence. While performing is not the only thing you have to do, without it, you are just putting lipstick on a pig!

Now, while this advice may be given with the best of intentions, it has some unintended consequences. While I am all in favor of hard work and perseverance, there is something to be said for **being noticed**. Whether in school or at work, people are often encouraged to *not* be noticed.

I often hear people say things like: "Flying under the radar screen is easy. It's less stressful blending into the crowd. If I blend in, no one will ever know if I made a mistake." Well, that may be true, but you'll be making headway and contributions as an anonymous donor as well!

There's nothing wrong with humility. In fact, we could all use a little more of it these days! Humility is key to allowing us to stay grounded yet to continuously attract people to us.

While people may gravitate toward the big personality, they only stay around if they don't feel completely drowned out and overwhelmed by it. Like a moth, they want to be drawn to the flame, yet not be consumed by it. However, humility is not the same as leaving your name off of your homework. I believe that good work should be noticed, and I believe that if you're going to do work at all, do good work.

Shrinking from the spotlight sends the wrong message. It tells others that you're not proud of your work or of your contribution. Maybe you're not even proud of yourself. It screams, "I'm not worthy" and we both know better than that.

What's more, being a shrinking violet is a habit and, as we all know, habits are hard to break. When you shrink from the spotlight, when you keep your head down all the time, you miss the best of life's precious opportunities. That's not what humility is about.

There's a line in the great movie *Training Day* that I love. It's uttered by the best bad guy you love to hate, but hate to love, played by the one, the only, Denzel Washington. Surrounded by other bad guys, knowing he's outnumbered, outgunned and outsmarted, Denzel's character tries to bluff his way out of the situation. Just before finding out whether he'll live or die, but suspecting he's probably on his way out, he shouts, "King Kong ain't got nuthin' on me!" (Well, that's the edited version, anyway.)

It's the ultimate spotlight moment because, in that instant, his character really believes he's King of the Hill, even when the ants start tearing him to pieces.

I'm not saying to bluff your way through life, or even worse, "fake it 'til you make it," but I am saying that you have to value yourself and be counted. Sometimes, when the entire world is telling you to sit down, you have to believe in your instinct to stand up and be counted.

We all need a healthy dose of bluster and confidence in our lives. If we want others to believe that we are valuable, that we have something to contribute, then *we* must believe it first. If we don't care enough about ourselves to stand up and stand out, then why should anyone else? I have watched people learn this lesson the hard way, many times before.

I Can't Want It More Than You Do

I have spent a lot of time during my career volunteering my time to assist small businesses. I like working with passionate people who have unwavering belief in their future success. I also like watching an individual, someone who has launched a great concept and is going through the growing pains of transforming it into a sustainable enterprise. As much fun as this can be, sometimes the pieces just don't come together.

One person in particular was an individual that we will call "Kelly." Kelly had a desire to start an eatery. Having done a great deal of research, she aggressively launched her concept. She found partners and investors who believed in the concept and brought it to life. Now, the ability to actually get off of the couch and launch a business has to be commended. Most people want to start a business. They want to be rich. They want to try something new, but they will never take any steps to make it happen. They will never move from want to action.

Well, Kelly definitely moved into action. She worked hard to open an establishment that had the ability to attract both a collegiate and professional crowd. There was just one thing missing: no one knew about the business.

Kelly put all of her energy into doing the good work of launching and running the business, but did not stand up to tell anyone about it. When you are running a small business, you have to be willing to tell anyone and everyone about it. Just like when you have a new-born baby – and you can't resist telling everyone who has an ear, how beautiful your child is. You need to communicate that same passion for a new business.

Kelly came to me looking for advice and ways to generate traffic. The problem, however, was that I could only be as committed to bringing people in the door, as she was. She had to be willing to step outside of her comfort zone and aggressively go after clients.

Whether it was showing up at festivals, marketing to local office buildings, or broad mass market advertising, Kelly needed to go get people. If she was not willing to stand up for her own businesses survival, why should I? What's more, if she wasn't willing to stand out from a crowd of other local eateries, why should anyone bother making a detour in her direction?

While you may not think you are running a business like Kelly, you actually are. Your career is the most important business you need to build. The more you invest in it, the more return you get from it. By standing up and letting people know how great you are, you are telling people, "This is a business you need to take notice of." It has been invested in, cultivated and marketed well – all of the key components to a successful venture. But just like any other business, if you manage your career poorly, can you really expect it to be successful?

Greed May Not Be "Good," But Self-Confidence Is

So what does this all boil down to? Simply put, you need to be self-confident. You need to have an unwavering belief that you deserve to be successful, and if you are investing the necessary money, creativity, passion and time into developing yourself, why shouldn't you?

I was watching a video by a famous orchestra conductor who was a passionate advocate for the beauty of classical music. While classical music is not my first genre of choice to listen to, I appreciated his passion as well as the beauty and artistry of the musicians. One thing that the conductor alluded to was the need for leaders to have an unwavering belief in their ability to accomplish their goals. His goal was to convince everyone of the beauty of classical music. (I guess he succeeded with at least one person!) He believed wholeheartedly that, if given the chance, he could get the entire world to appreciate his favorite form of musical expression.

The passion with which he delivered his plea was almost mesmerizing. While I may not have fully adopted classical music, I definitely adopted his views on leadership. It was by force of will and pure energy that he was able to change minds. Without self-confidence, he would have lost the battle before he even started.

Watch the Shade Trees

Now, I'm quite sure someone is reading this and thinking: here we go, another arrogant "arse" trying to justify his own ego. Well, anyone who knows me would attest that I am not short on confidence. And, yes, at times I have been too full of myself and moved from self-confidence to arrogance. Remember those inhibitors I mentioned last chapter? Well, one of mine is my self-confidence. While it is often one of my greatest assets, when unchecked it tends to push people away. If you are constantly hogging the spotlight, others will find it hard to realize their potential. While this may not be an intended consequence, it often happens.

Let's take into account one of my favorite individuals I have ever worked with: we'll call her "Dillard." Dillard is a very successful financial services executive in her own right. She grew up as an analyst in Investment Banking and more than held her own. When I was forming an internal Mergers and Acquistions group for a business unit I worked in, I thought Dillard would be an excellent addition to the team. I knew she was intelligent, quick, and had a strong enough personality to deal with me! Over the several years we worked together, Dillard proved to be a consummate professional with loads of potential. Her performance allowed her to progress to the position of Senior Vice President pretty quickly at the firm.

Despite her great performance, there was one catch: some people could not separate her success from my own. Some even thought that her success was somehow tied to me. Now, this could not have been further from the truth. In fact, I owe Dillard for *my* success.

If not for her dedication and partnership, we would not have accomplished nearly as much on our team. The issue came to light fully when I left my position in Mergers & Acquisitions to pursue a new business Profit / Loss (P/L) role. When I decided to leave, everyone assumed that I would take Dillard with me. Luckily, she and I had both realized that our careers were becoming too intertwined and it was time for a professional break. I think being out from under my cover allowed Dillard to fully develop into her own professional persona. Not having any shade allowed her to put her own unique brand on projects and deals. She was able to refine her own voice, her own style and, above all, her own swagger.

So, what about you? Are you feeling confident yet? If so, here are four questions that we all need to think about when it comes to managing our own self confidence:

1. **Do I love me enough to be myself?** If you don't love yourself, who will?

2. **Do I know why I should be confident?** What makes you special?

3. **Am I doing too much?** Is my ego out of control?

4. **Who am I stopping people from seeing?** Are they people that I want to help?

We should all care about the downstream impacts of our actions. If we don't care, we may wake up and realize that people can only see us because there is no one left around.

CHAPTER SEVEN

Make Your Own Path

"Two roads diverged in a wood, and I,
I took the one less traveled by,
And that has made all the difference..."
~ Robert Frost, *The Road Not Taken*

W e each have a path in life, a route that we travel from birth. For better or worse, our path in life is largely set in our childhood. Our parents' values, our race, our socioeconomic status, even our friends and colleagues, highly influence our path. The path we begin is often patterned by those we watch and with whom we interact. Like my young son, who used to literally try to walk in my shoes, we often try to follow in the footsteps of others.

We like this path because it's familiar, because it's a safe and predictable life. Most of us take our little twists and turns along our journey, for better or worse, but we often find ourselves right back on the beaten path. As the excerpt from this Frost poem indicates, however, we stay on the beaten path at our own peril.

One of the events that steered me toward my own path when the woods diverged was when I read *Why Should White Guys Have All the Fun?* by Reginald Lewis (Black Classic Press, 2005). While I did not try to become Reginald Lewis, his story opened up another world of possibilities to me.

Reginald Lewis was born into a somewhat tough neighborhood in Baltimore, Maryland. He had a strong family influence and began his "career" at age 10 with a local paper route. He tucked every penny he could save into a tin given to him by his grandmother, who had taught him the importance of saving out a portion of everything he made.

In high school, Lewis excelled at sports and academics, even while working evenings helping his grandfather as a waiter and maitre d'. He stayed busy and worked hard, and later, went on to attend Virginia State University on an athletic scholarship. After that, he attended Harvard Law School.

After graduating with his law degree, Lewis opened up the first African American-owned law firm on Wall Street. He specialized in corporate law, and wrangled significant deals for dozens of Fortune 1000 and, later, Fortune 500 and even 100 companies before entering into a few business deals of his own. One of those deals was for the McCall Pattern Company in 1983, and later the international division of Beatrice Foods.

From brokering deals for his clients to "doing the deals himself," Reginald Lewis built a fortune from his humble beginnings. But he never forgot those beginnings, and started the Reginald Lewis Foundation in 1987. Tragically, Reginald Lewis passed away at the age of 50 after a short illness, but his legacy of entrepreneurism, capitalism, and giving back continues through his foundation and other good works.

Additionally his legacy lives on today through his own words. According to the website for the Reginald F. Lewis Museum of Maryland African American History and Culture, "Reginald F.

Lewis lived his life according to the words he often quoted to audiences around the country: 'Keep going, no matter what.'"

Reginald Lewis was an inspiration to me for many reasons, which are not all obvious. What impressed me most about Mr. Lewis was that he deliberately, and personally, chose the path that was right for him.

Lewis could have taken any number of journeys, given his humble beginnings. Like so many, he could have chosen sports as his destiny, or the hospitality industry, which had been so good to his grandfather. He could have pursued law, which became an early passion.

Instead, he took those early lessons about money that his family instilled in him and used them to create a massive empire of his own, an empire of great financial worth and also generous financial giving. Reginald Lewis is more than just a professional inspiration; he is a personal one as well.

I'm reminded of a story that his wife, Lolita Lewis, told a group of us during a Christmas party that summed up his unique journey. Having become an avid art collector, Reginald was at an auction, bidding on an original Picasso (yes, I said Picasso!). After a frenzied bidding "war," which he won, Reginald received a standing ovation from the crowd. From paper route to Picasso – now that's an individual path.

Don't Just Take Any Path: Create Your Own

What happens to a lot of people is that instead of creating an individual path , they get swept downstream by the currents of life. This downstream shuffle starts early, at home. Our parents are our earliest influencers. We learn manners – right and wrong how to ride a bike, even whom to vote for and why, from our parents. They form our earliest mindsets about life and the universe.

It continues in grade school, this great social experiment, where we're quickly placed into certain "tracks" that tend to define our futures if we're not careful, or at least purposeful. If we're placed in the slow track, that's where we tend to stay. Some of us are put in the fast track which also helps to sweep us along.

We also form close, strong peer groups around this time, relationships that greatly influence our world view – not just in the present, but in the future. If our peer group is interested in sports, we tend to be interested in sports as well. If they're interested in movies, or writing, or art, or theater, or finance or politics, we tend to absorb those interests and mirror them as well. (In some instances, we find another peer group that does share our similar interests.)

As grade school ends and college looms, we are perhaps more prepared to make our own life decisions, but we are still being pushed along by family, friends and societal pressures.

If we've been athletes all through school, shouldn't we pursue that track in life as well? Can we switch tracks at that point, from being a jock to improving our intellectual capabilities? Or, conversely, if we've been a reader and a thinker, how dare we consider branching out into a more physical career? If our parents are wealthy entrepreneurs, wouldn't they frown on us going into teaching? And so on. Our friends, peers and even our parents often want only the best for us, but only we can truly know what that is. The question becomes: are we willing to follow our own path, even if it's the one less traveled?

How to Go Left When the World Goes Right

From firsthand experience, I can tell you that following your own path is one of the hardest things that you can do. It's more than just the uncertainty that we all feel when we make a difficult decision, it's the struggle against what we see everyone else doing. It's tough to ignore the advice we receive from the individuals that tell us to take the safe route, especially when their advice has been on point before. It's painful to fight through the feeling that we are disappointing others when we do something that they can't quite comprehend or understand. But such is the life for those who are willing to forge their own path and go left.

While I have had several instances in my career where I had to "go left," I can't think of a better example than one that involved one of my truest friends LaMarr Jones: "LJ." Hailing from Dayton, Ohio, LJ entered Morehouse College expecting to get a degree in engineering. Growing up in Ohio, being an engineer was the way to go. He had successful family members that started off as engineers, so it made a lot of sense to him.

While he spent his first year at Morehouse going down the engineering path, he quickly realized that it was not for him, and decided to change his major to finance. Now, in hindsight, this seems like a very easy decision to make, but for a 19-year-old, having to tell your family that you are about to make a life-altering decision, that took a lot of guts.

It was clearly the right decision, as LJ flourished as a finance major. Not only did he earn excellent marks, but he also took on leadership roles, including President of the Morehouse Business Association. When it was all said and done, LJ left Morehouse and headed to Wall Street. Sounds like a good decision to me.

Fast forward a few years. Now, it was just after the internet bubble had burst and LJ has left his first job on "the Street." As he was trying to decide what to do next, he was evaluating several opportunities. Having always had a passion for asset management, he took the opportunity to pursue it.

In addition, he was exploring the possibility of going into private equity or reentering investment banking. While either of those would have been a logical choice, given LJ's background and experience (a finance degree, three years as an analyst in investment banking, an overseas assignment in London, and a promotion to Associate), he had a gnawing urge to explore something new.

A few summers before, we had started throwing parties under the moniker, GFC. Because of the massive support we were receiving, LJ believed that he could turn GFC into a profitable business. He believed that not only was there a market for party promotion, but that there were a few examples of promoters transforming into niche marketing firms. At first, we enjoyed the energy and appreciation from those guests that attended our events. We thought the fact that we could draw a crowd was a great success. However, we soon began to realize that the true asset we were building was the database of young, upwardly mobile professionals with significant incomes. That database had value to companies and advertising agencies alike. All we had to do was figure out how to monetize it.

So the decision LJ had in front of him was this: take the guaranteed money from Wall Street or venture out and start a new company from scratch. Despite the very attractive financial offers coming in, LJ decided to follow his passion and turn GFC into a full-time, full-fledged business. This one act of following the unbeaten path has led to several unique opportunities.

From there, LJ launched event planning firms, urban marketing start-ups, and ultimately branched into the film industry. While his journey has been anything but easy, it has been a unique path that is his and his alone.

It's a path that he believes in; it's a path that he owns!

What's My Reward?

One of the biggest arguments for following the beaten path is the safety implied by the straight and narrow. You get a job, you work real hard, you let someone make your career decisions for you – when you'll get promoted, how much you'll make, what projects you'll work on, where you'll be relocated, etc. Ultimately, you are rewarded in the end.

But imagine if, 20 or 30 years ago, you'd let a company called Circuit City choose your path? What if that had been your "safety net," your straight and narrow, your beaten path? We can never forget that the ultimate responsibility for our lives rests with us. No one will care about your well being as much as you do!

Your Own Path Can Be Big or Small – Just Make It Personal

You've probably realized by now that this is not some "get rich quick" book, but rather a "find success on your own terms, in your own time, on your own path," book.

All success must be personal; big or small, rich or poor, success in school, in business, in money or in love must make sense to you, must fit with your own personality and ideals and, above all, must feel "right."

Anytime I've tried to go against my instincts, fought my nature or followed the "straight and narrow," I've wound up off of my own personal path, a place where I didn't feel authentic, couldn't do my best and had to succeed despite myself. It was a path not in line with myself.

I'm not saying that there won't be times in your life where you can necessarily choose your path. An entry level job? Your graduate school internship? A rigid deadline when you're eager to please? A first impression? There will often be situations where the straight and narrow is the only path available to you, but that doesn't mean that you can't do it your own way... just make sure it fits your journey.

And if you're finding yourself stymied too often where you are, stop being there. Find your own path, even if it's a challenge. The personal examples I've given display how I often had to go left when my career, or everyone else, insisted I go right. This chapter is about the path least taken, and often, that means leaving the world you know – the safe world, the beaten path, behind.

For you, your path might mean a:

- **new business you launch**
- **new product you create**
- **new initiative at work**
- **new way to meet clients; or**
- **new way to highlight your personal brand**

Sometimes, your own path will mean taking drastic measures; other times, it might mean tweaking the steps you're taking to gently merge into another lane. Regardless of the severity of change, if change is necessary, please don't be afraid to make it!

How to Guide Your Path

As you consider the path before you, and whether you want to keep going in the same direction or cut left or maybe right, or even up and down or back around – here are four questions to help guide you down your own personal path:

1. **What's original about my plan and path?** One way to indicate whether or not you're on the beaten path is to consider how original, unique, or even personal what you're doing is. I'm happy to say that we're in a time where entrepreneurs are popping up left and right, where the four-hour workweek is not so mythical, and where the career track often leads us to work from home, our own companies, or even abroad.

2. **How comfortable am I with being uncomfortable?** Before you answer this question, I have two words for you: risk tolerance. It's very important to weigh just how much risk you can tolerate on a daily basis. Jumping from one job to starting your own company on the same day can be a lot of risk to swallow, especially when it might take you six years to take a profit. Are you able to toil under that kind of pressure? We all seek comfort in our lives. For many, being "comfortable" is their definition of success, and more power to them. But for those who truly want a unique journey, get ready for the ride!

3. **What challenges am I likely to face?** Life is full of challenges and it is at its toughest when you are pursuing the path of most resistance! Before you go rushing down your own path, carefully consider the challenges you are likely to encounter. Don't be scared off by the obstacles, just get ready to jump over them.

4. **What are the benefits of going my own way?** Once you tackle the challenges you face, dig deeper and consider the benefits. Too often when confronted with change we think only of the negative, but I can tell you personally that my life has been both enriched and rewarded by following my instincts. Remember, it wasn't the fear of falling that got you riding your first bike, but the freedom of feeling the wind at your back...and the desire to catch up with your friends.

Regardless of the path you choose, these four questions can actually help you to make any decision a more practical, well-examined, and critical one. I have found these questions useful in decisions both big and small, and few decisions are bigger than deciding which path is the right one for you.

SECTION III

PLAY TO WIN

CHAPTER EIGHT

Can You Hustle?

"...look what I embody
The soul of a hustler, I really ran the street
A CEO's mind, that marketin' plan was me..."
~ Jay-Z, What More Can I Say

I f the brilliance in Benjamin May's quote is the yearning for each of us to stretch beyond our limits, the words of one of the greatest urban griots lets us know we must believe that we are, and can be, the best. It is not enough to release the fear of failure. We have to embrace our greatness. We must embrace the inherent greatness that resides in us all. We must believe that success is inevitable, if we are willing to put forth hard work, determination and effort.

We need this confidence to protect us like armor when the struggles of life bombard us. We need our belief to be resolute if we are to weather the intense storms of adversity that we all must endure along our road to greatness.

We must believe that each of us is here for a purpose and, unless we fulfill our unique and distinctive purpose, then our life is not fully complete. We must believe that unless we achieve our greatness, the world in some small way, will be shortchanged.

Who Doesn't Love the Underdog?

Maybe I'm a bit sappy this way, but I love a good underdog story. I love the story of the girl who beats the odds to do something remarkable, or the shaggy dog that walks 700 miles to find his home, or the 90-pound weakling who somehow triumphs over his bully.

That's why, as improbable as they sometimes seemed, I loved the *Rocky* movies. You know the story: guy from the wrong side of the tracks, who never could get a shot, finally gets a shot. He pours his entire life into that one shot. He trains, he sacrifices, he gives everything he has for that one opportunity. He doesn't have the fancy clothes, or the high-tech facilities, or even the time to train that his opponent does. He doesn't even fully understand how to do his job just yet. But he does have grit, determination, fire, drive, and desperation. Like the rapper Eminem said:

> *"Look, if you had one shot, or one opportunity*
> *To seize everything you ever wanted in one moment*
> *Would you capture it or just let it slip?"*

Whether it's *Rocky*, *8-Mile*, or *Rudy*, I guess I love the story of the underdog because, ultimately, it's my story. What I see on the screen is what I see in the mirror every day. The constant struggle, the fight, the persistence. Whatever Rocky has to endure, surmount or overcome, the underdog never lets the opportunity slip away. He doesn't always win, but he tries like hell!

The Boys of '97

What has always drawn me to underdogs is their ability to fight through the odds. It's the passion and drive that comes from knowing that every moment could be the one that changes your life. Every encounter could be the one that grants you an undiscovered opportunity.

In 1997, I moved to New York with a "rag tag" crew of individuals from Morehouse for our big shot on Wall Street: "the internship." Some of us had known each other for a few years, while we had just gotten to know the others in the group. We hailed from different parts of the country: from North Carolina to Washington and even a few from overseas.

While we came from various socio-economic backgrounds and experiences, we all shared a common thread: we were the underdogs. Above all else, that was what bonded us. While there were many people that we met and shared, with whom we had some great experiences that summer, the Boys of '97 for me will always be LJ, Robbie, Chris, Turp, Sullivan, KJ, and Scott. Without those guys' support, laughter and unconquerable spirit, things might have turned out very differently in my life.

Some of you may be saying right about now, "Well, Rod, you all came from a reputable educational institution and had already done well enough to secure a coveted place in the epicenter of financial wizardry: how could you all possibly be the underdogs?" My answer is very simple: statistically speaking, we didn't exist. The odds of making it to Wall Street are, in and of themselves, remote. But add to that scenario that the individuals involved were highly intelligent men of African descent, then the odds get even smaller, almost minute.

Then consider the fact that many of us hailed from families where, due to our economic situations, business and finance were like a foreign language, rarely spoken, let alone practiced, in the home. Take my own family, for instance. While a brilliant man of many talents, my dad never finished high school. Several of us hailed from true inner city communities, where just getting out – let alone getting to Wall Street – was a statistical improbability. So yeah, I'd say we were most definitely the underdogs on "The Street" that year!

81

For most of the Boys of '97, this was our first shot in the big leagues. Sure, many of us had done internships before and some had even worked in the financial sector during the academic year. We had all done a good job of understanding the academic side of business and had a little practice implementing it.

But 1997 was the ultimate test. While we all excelled at Morehouse (there were at least three Phi Beta Kappa graduates in our group), now we would have a chance to compete against the best and the brightest from across the country, even the world. We would be compared with the other interns from Penn, Harvard, Georgetown, and every other school. It was time to see how fast, even how far, we could swim.

Get Your Hustle On!

The first day we walked into our offices we all shared a sense of apprehension and excitement. This was it! Now what do we do? There were so many unknowns to conquer that first day; we didn't really know what to expect. We didn't know how we would be received. We didn't know the type of work we would be doing: making copies or running financial models.

We didn't know a whole host of things, but the one thing we *did* know was that we had to do – and would do – *whatever* it took to succeed. If that meant meeting different people inside and outside of our respective firms to figure things out: check. If that meant working 100 hours to get the work done: check. If it meant doing the grunt work like making copies, grabbing coffee, creating a phone directory or delivering packages to senior professionals: check, check, check and double check.

What it boils down to is we knew that we had to hustle because, for most of us, this was our shot! We knew that if we made a good impression that could solidify our futures on and off of Wall Street. Likewise, we knew that if we blew it now, our chances of making it back onto the Street would be slim to none.

And hustle we did. We leveraged every resource we could to gain an advantage. Many of the Boys of '97 were in a program called SEO: Sponsors for Educational Opportunity (SEO). SEO is a unique program that provides "superior educational and career programs to young people from underserved communities to maximize their opportunities for college and career success." Those of us that didn't belong to this select group still hustled our way into SEO events so that we could take advantage of the networking opportunities. To this day, many people assume that I was in SEO!

The same was true for those of us who were hired directly by Salomon Brothers, Goldman Sachs, Morgan Stanley, and Merrill Lynch. Whenever there were events that we thought we could get each other into, the word went out. It was this spirit of shared success that allowed us to survive the intensity of that fateful summer. This is a point that can not be stressed enough: our success was a shared success. When one person did something great, we all shared in that accomplishment because we'd all been a part of it. By having that collective force at our backs, it pushed us to do bigger and better things, both individually and as a group.

Work Hard, Play Hard

Part of learning how to survive in a high pressure environment is learning how to blow off some steam whenever, and as often, as you can. It's not just about goofing off; it's about taking the edge off so that you can bring your A-game every time. You have to learn to find some balance in your life. While that is always a challenge these days, it's something that we must all continuously work on.

As a bunch of 20- and 21-year-olds in New York City for a summer, you can imagine what form our "relaxation" took: partying. Not having much money, we were somehow still able to find many great places to party without breaking the bank. Whether it was house parties in Fort Greene and Park Slope or partying at Nell's, we always found a way to enjoy ourselves. We watched the July 4th fireworks by the Brooklyn Bridge – spectacular. We also threw our first (of many) summer bashes in the New York – even as interns, we wanted to take over the city! The social aspects of our experiences were invaluable to us. Not only did they strengthen our collective bond but it also allowed us to develop a strong network of individuals – we have treated each other as cherished friends ever since.

Whether it's the Hampton crew (Shelly, Ebony, Darryl); the Howard crew (Nigel, Kissonda, and many others); or the Georgetown crew (Sherrese), through our social efforts we were able to form significant personal *and* professional bonds (the lines often blurred) that continue to this day. Not only are there strong social ties, but we have done business together... now *that's* a good summer!

The Challenge

The need to hustle has been with me for a long time. But I remember the inflection point in my life when it became physically engrained in me. I have been a workaholic most of my life. I pulled my first all-nighter in the eighth grade. But up until then, schoolwork was the only place I put forth that type of all-or-nothing energy. That all changed the summer before my junior year in high school. I remember having a discussion with my mother about the upcoming school year and the car I had just bought, or was about to buy (a 13-year-old Plymouth Horizon that I loved). Maybe it was my cocky tone or the sense of entitlement that I was exhibiting, but my older brother, Eric, reacted; strongly. While it was well and good that I was excelling at school, he told me that day, that to excel academically was what I was *supposed* to do. It was not that big of a challenge, he said; everybody did it. He basically questioned whether I could handle my schoolwork if I had a job.

At the time, I was highly offended and was probably mad enough to see stars. How dare someone say I couldn't do something *and* excel. The reason it really struck home is the fact that I have looked up to my brother for years. He attended Morehouse College before me. He was the first person I remember wearing a French cuff shirt. He drove a clean red Honda Prelude. Eric wasn't just cool, he was the epitome of cool. But beyond that, he knew how to hustle. He always had a vision of what he wanted to do. Whether it was working at Eastern Airlines, promoting a concert or being a Chief Financial Officer, he knew how to give 100 percent to everything he set out to accomplish.

So, when the guy who epitomized hustle , questioned mine, the game was was on. Within weeks, I got a job working at the local library. I even ramped up my involvement in school activities.

Not only did I continue to play academic games, I joined the student senate, served as the junior class Vice President and ramped up my involvement in ROTC. The nudging Eric provided before that fateful year began to help me realize that I had a lot more that I could do and accomplish if I was simply willing to push myself beyond my comfort zone.

And you know what? Eric is still pushing me to this day.

He was one of the catalysts for forming the Urban Renaissance Growth Empowerment (URGE) movement, an organization focused on providing exclusive resources to entrepreneurs who would not have access to the talent level of professionals who work in management consulting, corporate America, or on Wall Street.

Never Stop Hustling

The principles of being the underdog have stuck with me throughout my career. It's that feeling of having a little something extra to prove that has kept me sharp, regardless of my past successes or former accomplishments. It has helped keep the fire burning inside of me – which is so necessary to help me continuously grow and develop. It has allowed me to match the grueling pace that financial services can often require with energy and enthusiasm.

The desire to stretch and learn compelled me to raise my hand to help lead the training program for the new analyst class. I figured if I could teach someone else the intricacies of modeling, then I would only get better at it myself. The desire to prove I could do it, gave me the courage to accept the challenge of working on the largest deal announced in history at the time: the failed merger of Worldcom and Sprint.

While the deal did not ultimately go through, the effort it took to pull off that kind of a deal – at that level, with those types of numbers, figures and A-players – was nothing short of herculean. The team collectively worked 30 days non-stop to get this deal ready. We modeled and modeled and modeled for weeks on end. There were even stretches where we lived in the office for three to five days straight. That deal was not for the faint of heart but, once we were done, I felt like a superhero!

That same spirit of hustle carries me forward to this day. When I talk about "hustle," I don't mean anything deceitful or shady. I think of hustle as energetic activity, an aggressiveness that allows you to push yourself and to shove past boundaries. Hustle is that x-factor that makes you stay a little longer, work a little harder, get up a little earlier, stay up a little later, shake one more hand, smile one more time, take one more pass through the final draft and generally focus on the details at which others barely glance.

Hustle is something we all need, now more than ever.

I believe that there are few things you can control in this world. You can't control if you are the smartest person in the room. You can't control if everyone likes you or not. Often you can't control the outcome of a challenging issue or problem. But what you can control is the amount of effort you put into **everything you do**. You can control how much energy you bring to the table, how "present" you are in any situation, whether you bring your A-game or your B-game, and whether or not you hustle.

When I think about solving issues with my clients, I owe them a certain level of energy and focus to get things done. When I work with our team, I owe them a certain level of energy and aggressiveness to help them remove any impediments to success. When I work with my mentees, I owe them a focused energy and empathy to help them think through their opportunities.

The energy you put forward says so much about you. It says what's important to you. It says what you value or don't value. It says what you are confident about. Even if you don't mean to give off these impressions, your energy does it anyway.

This is why I hustle. I hustle to let everyone know what I care about, what I value. I hustle because I need to make sure that those that follow in my footsteps have an easier path to get to where I am: so that they can greatly exceed anything I have accomplished. I hustle because to some degree I am still one of those Boys from '97 who knows that I only have one shot.

How Do You Hustle

Can you hustle? If so, how do you hustle? And why? Now it's time to ask yourself some real questions:

1. **Do you bring unbridled energy to the situations that you say you care about?** Hustling is all about energy, and those that have the most energy often get the most done. The challenge is in finding energy when you think the tank is empty. But it's a mindset, an attitude that says, "This is really important to me, so I'm going to be present for it." So in all situations, you have to find that motivating factor that increases your energy naturally; then you'll find that your hustle will follow.

2. **Have you really pushed yourself to the limits and then found a way to go beyond?** Comfort is a crutch. Getting somewhere and thinking that's as far as you can go is the quickest way to hitting a plateau and never moving beyond it. Hustling is about setting goals, reaching them, and then immediately setting a new goal that's just beyond that finish line you never thought you'd reach. That's how to stay sharp and keep your edge no matter what the situation.

3. **Do you view every opportunity given to you as your last chance to "make it happen"?** So many times I see successful people rest on their laurels to the point where they sabotage their own success. They get complacent in their talents, they don't keep up on their skills, they underestimate the competition, and they suffer as a result. When you hustle, every day is a new day; every opportunity is your last chance to prove yourself, and you truly are only as good as your last success. That kind of thinking keeps you sharp, on edge, and up to the challenge.

4. **Have you ever been backed into a corner, but instead of giving up, you came out swinging?** All of us fear defeat; it's human nature. But hustlers simply refuse

to accept defeat. Even when every indicator says otherwise, they will put their dukes up and keep fighting. Whether the challenge is internal or external, personal or professional, a true hustler will fight until his or her dying breath to overcome the obstacle. If they can't go above it, they'll go around it; if they can't go around it, they'll go under it. They'll find a way, because that's what hustlers do.

I could probably go on and on with questions, and even answers. I feel very passionately about bringing your A-game every day. It's more than just your raw intellect and abilities that will determine your success. Without passion and energy, it may end up being merely unfulfilled potential.

When I think about how I want to be perceived, it comes down to this:

*"I may not be the smartest or most intellectually gifted person in the room. I may not be the most talented player at the table. But one that I will have is the hustle. I will **never** be outhustled!"*

89

CHAPTER NINE

Playing the Game – Work Your Network (or Connecting Your Circle)

L et's just get this out of the way: I am not the best networker on the planet. If you define networking as being able to saunter into a room, meet 10 or 20 people and walk out with 10 or 20 meaningful long lasting relationships, then I am worse than bad; I'm horrible. I know many people have this conception of a politician style networking of "working a room" and "kissing babies."

But is this what networking is really all about?

When I hear complaints along the lines of, "I'm a people person at heart, but I really hate networking," I automatically think that this is the individual's perception of what networking is all about. What people are really saying when they tell me this is that they don't like playing this particular game of networking. They are saying, "This just doesn't feel natural at all." You know what? If this is what you think networking is, I completely agree.

People get frustrated by frequent superficial meet and greets, and the impersonal nature of LinkedIn and other social media sites.

Because of this frustration, they look at managing people's perceptions of them as an onerous full-time job.

But all business is networking, to some extent or another. All business is managing people's perceptions and, to some extent, personal branding across a wide variety of platforms. So how do we redefine networking so that it's more natural and something people can "get"? This is the reality of modern business and if you're not networking or managing perceptions, then you're playing to lose.

But that's not you. If you're here, if you're in the game, if you're already playing – why not play to win?

Evolving from Networking to Connecting Circles

When people tell me they hate networking, I immediately think, "So do I!" But the catch is that I don't consider what I do to be networking. I don't politic and I don't kiss babies. I like to think of what I do as "connecting circles." The world is full of people who have their own unique circles of influence that they live and thrive in. What I like to do is figure out how to connect my "circle" with their "circle."

In order to connect the circles, you have to first establish a personal relationship. This is the core of why most people hate networking they never attempt to make a personal link with other people. That's why they can say they're a "people person" in one breath and tell me they "hate networking" in the next. From these statements it's clear to me that they were not looking to make a personal connection in the first place. Making a connection is all about building relationships with people. So let's stop networking and start connecting circles!

One reason I believe people shy away from establishing real connections is that they require so much work. They require listening, understanding, effort, even compromise. What happens with most people when they talk about "networking" is they picture, or even practice, quantity over quality. The sheer enormity of "servicing" a network of more than a dozen or so people can be intimidating when you come at it from that philosophy.

But for me, connecting circles is a very personal experience. If you can't devote the time to relationships, then it's always going to be about "collecting business cards." But if you are connecting circles instead, the focus will be on working to earn trust and respect.

Let me give you an example of a young man, we'll call him "Mike," who has connected with my circle. Mike is a very intelligent and ambitious young man. He was introduced to me by a family member who is good friends with his family. Mike attended a celebration that my wife and I held at our home one summer.

Now, I can imagine Mike might have been very nervous or anxious, and possibly intimidated by our potential interaction. However, what I saw was a young man with a great demeanor. He spent the evening talking to my wife, my family, and other associates that I had invited to the event. Never once did he attempt to talk about business or ask for my advice right out of the gate.

Instead, he focused our first interaction on connecting with my circle. I was so impressed by Mike that I forced him to talk a bit about himself and his background before the evening was over. Because Mike found a way to make a personal connection, I was more than happy to talk about his career choices and opportunities and to provide any insight that I could. Mike has won half the battle; entering a powerful new circle of influence. Now it's up to us to maintain that connection into the future.

Remember: just like a good conversation, a good relationship is full of give and take. Often people completely miss this point. They always expect to "get" something from a networking experience, but are never prepared to "give" anything away. But remember, all points on a circle are connected, so anything that you give will come back to you (and anything you take will come back to you as well!).

Substance is Key to Maintaining Your Circles

The crux of anything we do should be to develop something meaningful, something of substance. Too often we associate networking with crowded Chamber of Commerce events, alumni receptions, or conferences where everyone is wandering around, shaking hands, and "pitching," and nothing much of substance ever gets shared.

I think of connecting circles as "dinner for two" rather than a cocktail party. Even if it's done in a crowded room, focusing on one person at a time, giving them your undivided attention, listening, hearing, translating, sharing, understanding and then delivering on your promises and following through on the discussion, these are the building blocks of a good relationship, a good circle.

But it all starts with substance. Building your inner circle, one trusted partner at a time, leads to opportunities that put your substance to work. That is the true spirit of connecting circles: gaining momentum and contacts, by delivering substance at every stop along the way.

So let's take a look at how making a meaningful connection has benefited my career. When I first started interning at Salomon Brothers, I had the good fortune of interacting with various talented individuals. One in particular was a gentleman named Lewis. At the time, Lewis was a Director in the Mergers and Acquisitions group where I was working. Over the course of the summer, he witnessed my hard work and desire to improve and he provided me helpful guidance. When I returned to the firm as a full-time analyst, Lewis and I continued to build a strong working relationship. I even worked on a few projects for him during my time in Mergers and Acquisitions. During the course of my time overseas and eventually working in other parts of the firm, we remained in close contact.

At one point about five or six years after I started at the firm, I was considering exploring other opportunities. I had spent a lot of time advising companies on acquisitions and raising capital, but I wanted to shift my focus to one company in a corporate strategy role. I began looking at a few opportunities externally and was becoming more serious about making a move. At the same time, Lewis was contemplating making a similar move internally. The firm was forming a new business and Lewis was going to head the Mergers and Acquisitions team to focus on growing the business through acquisitions. He told me they were forming a new strategy team as well and looking for people with an investment banking background.

I thought the opportunity sounded very interesting and, even though I had heard some mixed reviews about the business, I knew and trusted Lewis. Lewis's referral was critical to my getting the role. It was this role that served as the catalyst for my career acceleration that ultimately led me to the position of Managing Director. Had I not made that connection with Lewis years before, I would probably not be writing this book today.

The circles we connect are like planted seeds. We have to constantly nurture them, even when we're busy or tempted by shinier objects, never really knowing exactly when or how they might bear fruit at some later date. But when we harvest them at the right time, the fruit is very sweet indeed!

Mentors Versus Sponsors

What's better: a mentor who provides guidance or a sponsor who can get you paid and promoted? The fact is, both are critical depending on your own individual path.

You can't just discount mentors because they are often more spiritual advisors than paid promoters. The fact is, a good mentor can put you in a better place, a more grounded, wise and informed place, where you'll be better able to attract the eye of a solid sponsor.

Likewise, finding a sponsor to promote or even hire you into a new position, can help you work alongside, or even for, powerful mentors who can take your career and mental game to the next level.

Regardless of who you're speaking to, building relationships should always be about developing who you are. Even if you're standing in place at the moment, you should always be working, always be striving, to improve who you are so that you can continue on your journey with constant forward motion.

Unfortunately, most networkers ignore this truism. They want the company CEO to be their mentor, right away. They want the Managing VP of Corporate Affairs to be their sponsor, immediately. The odds of that happening, however, are astronomical, so they merely give up and move on to the next pipe dream. The fallacy is that those networkers were not ready to make a personal connection with those individuals. The best they could have done was take something from those individuals, but what did they have to give in return?

Making a true connection is about laying groundwork through delivered promises, met expectations, and delivering substance. When it's done effectively, the connections you develop become strong bonds that you will be able to leverage time and time again in the future.

Who is Your Personal Advisory Board?

One of my most effective networking methods, beyond delivering substance in every personal and professional relationship, is having what I call a personal advisory board.

This "board" may be made up of your first boss, an old college roommate who has gone on to be quite successful in their chosen profession, the VP of international sales and marketing for your company, or a trusted clergyman, neighbor, former teacher, or spouse. It can be composed of young people, older people, men, women, experts from different fields, and members of all professions.

This advisory board is informal, of course. There is no board room, no long table with leather chairs, but it works just the same for me. It consists of my closest, most respected, and influential mentors and sponsors. I consider them a "board" because I hold them in elite status and consult with them frequently, much as you might a corporate or professional advisory board. The meetings may be informal, but the discussions, the advice, the questions and answers, and even the feedback I'm often given is most certainly not.

It's important to populate your board with people you trust, but also people who aren't necessarily your biggest cheerleaders or fans. Don't get me wrong; these should all be supportive people, but they should not be "yes men" or "yes women," who are there just to pat your back and to tell you that everything you do is right or glorious.

The main goal of having such a board is to solicit feedback from its members. That means being open to positive (of course) and negative feedback. Feedback helps you to define your performance and shed bad habits and even emotional deadweight.

The truth can hurt, and it's often discouraging to learn that yes, actually, our crap does stink! But knowing our weaknesses often helps us turn them into strengths, and that is one of the most valuable uses of your own personal advisory board.

One more thing: remember to keep your board fresh. Like any good organization, no one needs to be on your board forever (well, maybe, except for your spouse). It's a great idea to find new voices to hear and people to learn from. Periodically adding and subtracting people from your board prevents you from becoming to stagnant and complacent. New ideas and perspectives are critical to not getting stuck on your journey.

The Golden Rule: *Be the Mentor or Sponsor You Want*

The Golden Rule states that we should "do unto others as you would have them do unto you." I can't think of any better mantra for entering into a mentor or sponsorship relationship than those achingly truthful words.

You have to learn to give to get! Seriously, you must be willing to give as much as you get in **any personal relationship**, particularly when you are seeking guidance and wisdom from a mentor, or job assistance, even monetary assistance, from a sponsor.

I often find that, in my role as a mentor or sponsor to others, it helps me understand what my own mentors and sponsors do on a daily basis, why they do it, and even where they're coming from.

Understanding comes from being on both sides of the fence, and learning to merge with either experience equally. Being mentored and/or sponsored is a wonderful experience, but I think being a mentor or a sponsor is even more rewarding.

Mentoring or sponsoring others not only helps others, but enlightens you as well. Sorting through their various issues and challenges helps evolve your own thinking about how to solve and work through situations. I find that the more I mentor and sponsor, the more I tend to model my own behaviors, advice, even my own wisdom and guidance, on a kind of "Ideal" sponsor or mentor that I wish I had.

This helps me to interact both with my own mentors and sponsors as well as with those I'm mentoring and sponsoring myself. Knowledge isn't just power, it's enlightenment, and knowing how to mentor/sponsor others enlightens me on how to be a better "student" to those who honor me by being my mentor or sponsor.

Questions for Connecting Circles Like a Winner

As you continue to refine the way you build personal relationships, as well as your circle itself, here are some thoughtful, probing questions to ask along your own journey:

1. **Do you practice making connecting circles?** Building relationships is actually a journey within our journey. It's not an event that you do, without fail, time and time again, but a process we learn from – if we're careful – every time we do it. So, this leads to a few more questions: Is this something you're already engaging in? If so, are you continually trying to improve the way in which you attempt to connect circles? If you're not already building relationships, why not? Asking these questions, even if you consider yourself a master networker, can lead to thoughtful, even surprising or challenging answers.

2. **Are you cultivating the world's perceptions of you?** Every time you make a connection, it's an opportunity to mold, craft or even cultivate how the world thinks about you. If you network like a "business card collector," you

are molding perceptions of just another opportunist on the prowl. However, if you network with purpose, with follow through and substance, you become a trusted ally that others can refer or recommend with trust.

3. **Who are you mentoring?** We often think that mentors are people there "for" us, not ourselves. The fact is, mentoring is a valuable networking method, and not just to take from but to give back. When we mentor we help others and ourselves.

4. **Who is on your board of advisors?** As I discussed, it's a really good idea to have a trusted personal board of advisors to help mentor and sponsor you along your own vital path to success. But having a board with the wrong members is almost as useless as not having a board at all. Don't just fill your board with backslappers, do-gooders and "yes men." Instead, staff it with trusted folks who aren't afraid to play "devil's advocate" and make you aware of the shortcomings of a plan or an opportunity, or even your own shortcomings.

5. **Do you know how to use them?** Feedback from your personal advisory board is a vital tool for helping guide you along your path, but only if you're skilled in hearing, and accepting, that feedback. Avoid "kneejerk" responses when advisors tell you that something may be a bad idea, or that you're rushing things or the timing is right or even that you're not ready for a significant position or opportunity yet. You chose these "advisors" for a reason; now you just have to learn to trust them as well.

The most important rule in networking, or connecting circles, is to simply be genuine. People can smell insincerity a mile away. If you want to make real connection, start with being real yourself!

CHAPTER TEN

No Substitute for Leadership

It's no secret that there are a lot of talented people in the world. We all have our unique gifts and characteristics, and there are those whose ability to empathize with their common man is both touching and amazing. We saw it every time Oprah Winfrey simultaneously touched the heartstrings of her guests, audience and viewers around the globe.

Others are just so intellectually gifted that we marvel at how their mind works, eager to tap into some of that unique and inspiring insight. The insights of the preeminent psychologist and pioneer in the development of an African-centered approach in modern psychology, Dr. Na'im Akbar, come to mind. Others still are creative geniuses whose ability to show us the future we don't even know we want, is uncanny. One look at the impact Apple has had on music, publishing and technology, solidifies Steve Jobs' place in the creative pantheon. There are those whose gifts stem from the genetic makeup of their physical attributes. We watched Michael Phelps and Usain Bolt dominate the 2008 Olympics and, four years later, the 2012 Olympics with seemingly superhuman feats.

Why are these people so personally and professionally inspiring? One reason we marvel at those individuals who we believe have a unique talent or gift is because it allows us to believe in our own unique talents and gifts. They allow us to dream, to actively visualize ourselves revealing our own hidden or not-so-hidden talents with the world. We can even fantasize about the gifts we possess. Who has not dreamed about winning an Olympic gold medal? Who hasn't dreamed that their "bright idea" was the one that was going to transform the world? We all have these dreams because they're fun, because they're satisfying and, above all, they give us something to strive for.

But wait: who dreams about being the leader? I don't mean who dreams about being President or some other famous politician. I mean, who dreams about being a *true* leader? Most of us stray from being leaders. It seems hard, too much work, too much stress, too much responsibility... it's just too much! But why are we so afraid? I believe it's because we really don't understand what leadership is and, rather than dig deeper, we simply avoid the whole scenario altogether.

A leader is defined as a person who "rules, guides or inspires others." While most individuals may focus on the rule of others (isn't that what people in charge do?), I think that the heart of it is the willingness to guide and inspire others.

Can't Wait 'Til I'm Older

For most of us, leadership is a confusing concept, at best, and an intimidating one, at worst. We learn some bad lessons about leadership from an early age that we have to overcome. When we were kids, we couldn't wait to become an adult so we can tell someone else what to do. As a result, we associate being in charge with "telling someone what to do." I can remember bristling as a kid every time my parents told me what to do, (especially when it was something I didn't want to do). I could not wait until it was my turn to be in charge. These days, I can even see my own son having the same reaction when somebody "bigger" tells him what to do.

This idea of what it means to be in charge is what most of us initially associate with leadership. Unfortunately, it is also the one idea about leadership that is the farthest from the truth. Because of our natural desire to control our own destiny, we strive to be the person in charge. It seems to make us feel better; it gives us more control. Unfortunately, the goal of being in charge is actually counterproductive to our development as leaders.

Being in charge is a designation someone else usually gives you. You are hired as the shift supervisor. You are hired as a manager. You are promoted to Vice President. While you may have worked very hard for this acknowledgement, the fact remains that it was still given to you by someone else. And therein lies a critical difference between perception and reality because leadership is something you have to accept yourself.

There are thousands of books and articles written on effective leadership, leadership styles, leadership traits, examples of leaders, the list goes on and on. I don't need to revisit what a leader looks like. But what we *do* need to discuss is what leadership is and why it matters.

What Leadership (Really) Is...

Leadership has nothing to do with being in charge. Leadership is about:

- having a vision and a willingness to help others to see it;
- listening to and learning from others so that you can collectively reach a goal;

- having the willingness to push toward a goal to make decisions, despite the possibility of failure;
- being accountable and responsible; and
- wanting to inspire others to be better and greater than they believed.

Ultimately, to truly lead we have to be willing to serve.

Followers Lead, Too

I have always been a bit of a rebellious sort. Now, that's not to say that I caused much trouble, but I have always been one to go against the grain. I just like the road less traveled, maybe because it's less crowded! I've been that way for as long as I can remember. When I was at Renaissance High School in Detroit, Michigan, this trait led me toward the Junior Reserve Officer Training Corp (JROTC). Most high school freshmen were not flocking to sign up to a class that required you to wear a green suit (my uniform) every week.

Now, my reasons for signing up were twofold:

1. My older brother James had been in the Army (a Green Beret, I think) and I used to love when he would send us letters from around the globe. (To this day, I still remember the papyrus he sent us from Egypt.)
2. I was a 5'1" freshman that weighed 115 pounds soaking wet, so the idea of physical education class (PE) just did not excite me. JROTC seemed a much better alternative.

Now, the whole idea of leadership is what initially interested me in the JROTC program. I thought this would be my chance to tell some people what to do. But I quickly learned that was not the case. Being a lowly private like any other freshman, I was at the bottom of the pecking order. I had to first learn how to listen and follow others before I lead anyone.

I guess the opportunity to be in charge outweighed my aversion to following orders because I actually stuck with it. I learned that if I was willing to listen, I could learn a lot from the older cadets and from our advisor, Sgt. Felton. And a strange thing happened: despite not being in charge, people started to listen to me anyway. They thought I had a few good ideas and actually wanted to hear them.

That's when it hit me: leadership was really about influence. It didn't matter if I was "in charge" or not. If I was influencing those around me, I was leading. I learned that even as a follower, I could still lead. That lesson has helped me throughout my life and career. And, by the way, I did end up in charge, after all: I was the City of Detroit Corps Commander my senior year!

Take Them to the Emerald City

People often write about the importance for leaders' vision. While it may sound cliché, if you don't know where you are going, how can anyone follow you there? Growing up, I did not have many examples of what success in the corporate context looked like, but I had an idea in my head of what it *could* look like – and that's what I went for.

The thing about vision is that it's not always a specific end goal or destination. Sometimes, it's a guide stick that shapes our decisions and choices along our path. That's the beauty of it. Because we are trying to create something that may not have been done, seen, or accomplished before, it *can't* be specific!

When I first moved to New York, I was putting a lot of time into launching my career and so were some of the other Boys of '97. We worked very hard and wanted a way to enjoy the social aspects of the city in what little time off we could muster. While we loved the energy of the city, we thought there was an opportunity to enhance the social experience for ourselves and the other diverse urban professionals we encountered.

So Bryan, LJ, Michael, Quincey, Robbie, and myself had the great idea for a new type of social experience: GFC. (What, exactly, GFC stands for is a discussion for another book). We wanted to create an environment where some of the most successful up and coming young professionals in New York could come together to relax and to blow off steam in an environment where they knew they were among family. We figured that if we could create a social environment we enjoyed, with people we wanted to be around, then others would follow.

We initially focused our energies around an annual summer bash that would set New York ablaze. For four summers in a row, we produced an event that not only attracted successful professionals, but attracted celebrities and people from all over the globe. That's right – people flew in from Asia for our events! What started as a simple idea turned into a legendary string of events that still conjure some of the best memories to this day.

Now, did we really know that people would respond positively to our social venture? Of course not. But we *did* know that something new and different was needed and that we were willing to take the risk. Like the statement in the movie *Field of Dreams*, "If you build it, they will come." And boy, did they!

This one foray into vision and leadership expanded the perception of what we could accomplish. This led to new career directions for some, and the forming of several new ventures – from event planning to marketing, to film – for others. While there was varying success amongst these activities, the ability to envision "what could be" never went away.

Take One for the Team

When I first started to manage projects and, ultimately, people, I was more comfortable with the work I did versus everyone else's. I knew the quality of the work I produced, and was willing to stand up for it. I was young and inexperienced and had to learn how to trust people. As I became more comfortable with delegating tasks, I was faced with a new challenge: what happens when other people mess up? More importantly: what happens when people mess up and you don't catch it?

Well, that was a whole new wrinkle that I hadn't quite bargained for. I was okay with delegating tasks so long as the work was perfect (the gold standard I always held myself up to), but if they could not get it right, why give it to them? Moreover, was I supposed to take the fall for their mistakes? Hey, wait a minute now; *I* didn't mess up!

The first time I was faced with this issue was during an acquisition deal I was working on in Europe. We had spent several months doing due diligence on buying a unique business that spanned eight different countries. The team had spent tireless weeks scouring through documents to assess the risk and opportunities for the business. As with any acquisition, we were required to give frequent updates to the senior management about how the deal was progressing. These reviews tended to be very thorough and intense, all in an effort to make sure that we assessed the opportunity accurately. The team would develop robust financial models to analyze the data and attempt to forecast how lucrative the acquisition could become.

On this one particular deal, a key member of our team missed a key fact about a liability that could negatively impact the deal... to the tune of over 50 million dollars! Now, while this particular area of diligence was not my direct responsibility, ultimately, I was responsible for the entire deal. That meant that anything we accomplished or failed to find *was* my responsibility. Needless to say that when I found out about the "miss," I went pale (which is kind of hard for a black guy to do!).

I had a few options:

1. I could put my head in the sand and act like it didn't happen (this option probably would have gotten me fired);
2. I could disclaim all responsibility and blame the person who missed it (this option probably would have been career limiting for the individual and I would have lost all respect I had earned at the firm);
3. Or, I could work with the individual to find a solution to our 50 million dollar problem.

I chose the third option. I had to step up to the plate and take responsibility for the team's miss and, though it was painful and uncomfortable, I learned a valuable lesson: people respect individuals who shield their team from pain and punishment. As the leader, you get the benefit of your team's success, so you also have to be able to bear the brunt of the problems when they arrive.

As a result, your team will respect you because they know you are in it with them and, surely enough, the organization as a whole will respect you, too. Now, there are limits to how far you should take this – illegal and immoral actions should never be shielded. But a good, old-fashioned honest mistake is something we all make.

Your ability to be both accountable and responsible, even when challenges arise, is a critical characteristic of a leader. Besides, who wants to follow behind someone that ducks every time a ball is thrown their way? Since they expect to get hit, they will never warn you when you can't see it coming.

Just Decide Already

Have you ever wondered why things never get done? People find it very hard to come down on one side of the fence or the other, whether in their personal or professional lives. I think that is because people hate to make decisions.

We all feel just a little better when we can pass the decision making buck on to someone else, and very few of us like to be the ultimate authority when it comes to a hard and fast decision. While it's easy for most people to play "armchair quarterback" and say what they would or wouldn't have done in any particular scenario, it can be nerve wracking to actually decide what you would have done.

We all run through those "disaster scenarios" where we choose to go with that company, that provider, that business partner or to hire that person who turns out to be the company/provider/partner/ employee from hell and, of course, **it's all our fault**!

One critical skill set all leaders must employ is that of decisiveness. Decision making is a skill we could all use more of, but for leaders it's not simply a luxury but a necessity.

Whether you are in charge of many people or just one person, several projects or just a single one, your ability to make clear, focused, informed and intelligent decisions will help you lead with authority and skill.

Ultimately, decision making isn't just about making arbitrary, personal or even professional choices. It's about listening to and learning from others so that you can collectively reach a goal together.

We All Want to Be Inspired

Decision making is an active trait, something you must think about consciously and regularly to ensure that you're making the right decisions for the right reasons. But inspiration is something you just do; or are.

All leaders must inspire both consciously and subconsciously. It is an unwritten skill set, something that is hard to teach or even impart to others, but something you must do almost as background noise, even when you think nobody's actually watching.

One way to inspire others is to lead by example, which is how I've been personally and professionally inspired in the past. When I see a true leader at work, when I am blown away by his or her leadership style, dedication, passion or brilliance, I immediately want to do better myself.

Most of us are like patchwork puzzles, working on ourselves one aspect, one trait, one part of a skill set at a time. One quarter can be all about dedication, another quarter, attention to details, another, our people skills and another, our self-confidence. Gradually, over time, we amass our own skill set that others, hopefully, wish to emulate.

As you go about working, and leading, keep an eye on yourself. Ask yourself, "Is this inspiring to others? Am I at my personal and professional best? If someone were watching this right now, would it inspire them to act, even lead, differently?"

Inspiration is also about passion; it's about joining people together in a common ideal, deadline, deliverable or goal that you can all participate in. Sometimes inspiration is passive, like when you lead by example. But other times it's very, very active, as when you are forced to kind of "rally the troops" with an old-fashioned, "let's win one for the Gipper" style speech.

In times of crisis or even just ennui, don't bore the troops with "I, me and my" statements but instead speak to the collective "we." Touch team members where they live and extol the virtues of the project to ensure that you are all on the same team, even if you are still their fearless leader.

Why Is It So Hard?

Leadership is not easy. It's not something you master overnight, if you ever do. It's a lifelong process that always seems to be refining itself, evolving and shaping into something new, different and distinct each time you are faced with a unique challenge or obstacle. So give yourself a break if you don't exactly feel like the President of the United States (POTUS) at this very moment!!!

Still, there are some questions you'll want to ask before you assume any leadership role, starting with this one: do you want to be a leader or just the guy they put in charge? Your answers to the following questions will be your ultimate answer:

1. **Do you want the prestige associated with the title and business card or are you willing to put the work in?** Position, title and having the corner office are the least indicative trappings when it comes to a leader's true ability to rally his team to deliver on a specific goal. What's more, if the trappings of leadership are all you aspire to, you aren't half as likely to do the real work of "leading" that makes leaders out of bosses.

2. **Do you know where you are going? Can you help others get there?** Leadership doesn't exist in a vacuum. You can read all the leadership books out there and take every seminar, but if you can't interact with others effectively, it will all be for naught. Leadership itself is a

team effort, and your principle goal of being a leader is to "lead" an assortment of others to one common goal, deliverable or purpose. Knowing where you are going is the first step toward enlisting others to follow you there.

3. **Do you have all of the answers?** If you think the answer is "yes," then I can categorically state that you are most definitely *not* ready to lead. That's because in order to lead effectively, you have to truly believe that you cannot be the smartest guy in the room every day. (If that's the case, you obviously need to fire everyone else.) When it comes to leadership, confidence *and* humility go hand in hand.

4. **Can you make a decision when the money is on the line?** You can't freeze when the pressure is on. You not only have to be willing and able to make decisions but you need to do it when the pressure is on. Earning the trust and admiration of your team, as well as trusting their allegiance to you and to the project, will help you to make collective and creative decisions quickly.

5. **Do you accept responsibility not only for your own mistakes, but for those of others?** Leadership isn't just about taking credit for the good decisions and placing blame for the bad; it's about accepting responsibility for both. Now, if you have enough credibility to accept the blame for someone else's mistakes, then you are on your way.

6. **Can you inspire others to follow you?** If you don't have any passion, no one will listen. People need to believe that you care, and this is something which you cannot fake.

So what did you all decide? Are you ready for leadership? I believe to some degree you are. Now the next step is to start practicing your leadership skills...today.

You never know – one day, I may be following you, too!

CHAPTER ELEVEN

Don't Put Your Head in the Sand — Get Back Up!

"Life for me ain't been no crystal stair."
~ **Langston Hughes, *Mother to Son***

The challenge with having good people around you who are willing to tell you the truth, is that they will actually **tell you the truth**. They won't just tell you what you want to hear, but what you *need* to hear. They do it because they actually care.

Like you, I am on a continuous journey. My family, my career, my experiences, this book… it all has been a journey. Sometimes on that journey, you have to stop and ask yourself (or someone else): "Am I being real? Am I being honest?"

In one of those honest moments with my wife Kaili, she made a poignant observation: "Have you really been able to have success in your career without having any real failures? Have you not had any major stumbles or setbacks? Has your career really been that easy? If so, why don't they come out in your story?"

I was stunned. Her observation forced me to honestly assess how I thought about my career journey. Was I just applying "spin" to my journey to make it seem like a charmed life? Was I reluctant to bare the pain in fear of becoming too vulnerable? Or was I just afraid?

It's Never as Easy as it Seems

My mother, Bobbie Helen Hardamon, was an educator in the public school system in Detroit for over 40 years. While she is well-educated and can be as hard-nosed as they come, she was also once a single mother and divorced. She raised three kids while pursuing a graduate degree, she made a way. She put three kids through college; she made a way. Whenever she thought I was taking things for granted, she would remind me of her favorite line in her favorite poem by Langston Hughes, *Mother to Son*, "Life for me ain't been no crystal stair."

Now, as a child, I didn't fully grasp what that line meant. I couldn't fully appreciate the sacrifices it takes to raise children and to go to school. I didn't grasp the opportunities that she might have given up. I didn't realize the financial burden of putting two children simultaneously through college.

Part of the reason I didn't fully realize these challenges is because my mother made it look so darn easy. No matter the struggles that went on behind the scenes at the time, everything always worked out in the end. She wanted to improve my comprehension, so my mother found a way to buy a computer in 1984. For a school trip to Montreal, she found a way for me to attend. When a family member needed a place to stay, she found a way to make room. She simply *always* found a way.

You see, my mother Bobbie only focused on the roadblocks enough to figure out how to overcome them. She learned from the challenges. They made her tough. They made her stronger. My mother could have easily adopted a "woe is me" attitude, because at the time, the odds were literally stacked against her. Instead, however, she asked, "If not me, then who?", and simply got it done! It is this kind of resolve and attitude that has stuck with me to this day.

Sometimes We Need Rose-Colored Glasses

So, in the interest of being completely transparent and truthful, let me set the record straight: I have had a few stumbles in my career. I have had setbacks and failures. There have been more than a few times when I thought that I messed up so badly that I would be fired. At the time, of course, I thought the world would end.

During my second year as an analyst I was assigned to work on a large telecommunications Mergers and Acquisitions deal. I was also working on a deal for one of the individuals who had really taken an interest in me, my man Ric. He taught me a lot about how to do deals and how to build relationships with clients. Ric is a fair, no-nonsense guy with a great sense of humor. Because I had done well on a previous deal for him, he gave me a lot of responsibility.

Well, the thing that I didn't quite understand when I took on the large telecommunications transaction was how hard it was going to be to juggle both deals at the same time. On the large deal, I played the normal analyst role, creating complex financial models. On Ric's deal, I was supposed to "step-up" and play the role of senior analyst. I was not only responsible for making sure that the work was done, but I was responsible for the quality control.

The problem was that working on the large deal called for working 20-hour shifts at a time, greatly reducing my ability to catch mistakes on Ric's deal. After a few weeks of royally screwing up and sending an error-ridden product to the client, Ric called me into his office and let me know how badly I was messing up. Not only was I crushed by the quality of my performance, but I felt like I was personally letting Ric down.

I literally thought I had ruined my career. I expected Ric to remove me from the deal right then and there and then run and tell everyone how horrible I had done. I thought it was over; all of it. I thought my reputation was toast. Instead, I made a choice to try to do everything I could to regain Ric's trust. I refocused my efforts and, after getting some help from the team, we were able to get back on track. I ended up not losing Ric's trust, and ultimately, I gained his respect. He knew that no matter how tough or how bad things got, I would not quit on him.

This story could have easily ended with Ric's message of failure, but that is only half of the lesson. You see, it's not that I don't have issues, I just choose to focus on what I learned from these experiences. How did it stretch me? How did it make me stronger?

I choose to focus on what I gained and learned and not simply where I failed. I purposely choose to wear rose-colored glasses. I choose to focus on the positive aspects of my life and my experiences.

I believe in breathing life into the positive things you would like to do on your journey by speaking about them. Words are an amazing form of energy that shape the direction we travel. You know what they say: be careful what you ask for because you just might get it. If you dwell on the negative, then you get more thunderstorms. If you dwell on the positive, I believe you get more rainbows. And we all know that you find a pot of gold at the end of the rainbow.

Setbacks Happen ... Get Over It

If you think every moment in your life will be smooth and free of trials and tribulations, you might as well just close this book now because you have missed the point. Life is rough and tough. Success does not come easy. It is not for the faint of heart. It takes self-reflection and introspection. It takes hard work and perseverance. It takes a strong foundation and moral grounding. And even if you have all of these, you will still have setbacks and road blocks. You need them to continuously learn and grow.

Now, when I made the position of Managing Director at age 31, I did not quite know what to do. I was having a wonderful career at Citi. I loved doing strategic deals and buying, and I had become pretty good at it. Now, while I loved being a deal guy, I noticed I was not the decision maker. I could provide wonderful strategies and ideas to the business heads I advised. I could drum up wonderful analysis to make some very convincing arguments. But ultimately, it was someone else's decision, which I did not always agree with. I decided then and there that, on my particular journey, I wanted to be a decision maker: I wanted to run a business unit.

If I had my druthers, I would have walked right out of my role as Co-Head of Mergers and Acquisitions to a plush business head role, but alas, that was not my wave. I had recently led the firm in its $1.45 billion acquisition of BISYS Group, Inc. BISYS was a leading provider of fund accounting services to mutual funds, hedge funds and private equity funds. Having literally spent several years hunting this opportunity, I had become very familiar with the business. Because I thought it was a great addition to the firm, I decided to leave my role in Mergers and Acquisitions to be a senior member of the hedge fund business.

Notice I did not say that I was running the business. I came aboard to initially be a conduit between the management team that we had just acquired and the rest of the Citi organization. In addition, I was charged with helping the hedge fund business completely revamp its technology infrastructure. I put 100 percent into the role and, in a couple of months, I was asked to take over the entire integration of BISYS into Citi. While I worked hard leading the integration, when the business head role became available a few months later, the job went to someone else. I was disappointed. It was not that I thought that the other person wasn't qualified, it's just that I hate to lose. Again, I had a choice: fold or get better.

Well, I don't fold.

I decided to spend the next four years learning the business. I spent time with our operational and technology teams to understand what made our business tick. I spent time with alternative investment managers to better understand their opportunities and challenges to better enable us to deliver solutions that met their needs. I spent months studying, researching and listening to my team.

The learning curve was steep. The challenges were many. The successes were hard to come by, but I stuck with it. The hard work culminated in my promotion to the North America Head of the business. Did it occur exactly when I wanted it? No. Did it take a lot of effort? Absolutely, yes... but it *did* happen.

At some point you have to say, "I am not going to be defined by my setbacks and failures." At some point, you have to focus on winning!

Keep Moving Forward

When we experience the hard times in life, sometimes we all need a moment to regroup. We need to let the sting from our wounds heal. But once that healing is done, we all need to ask ourselves: how do we move forward? Asking yourself the following questions will help you to get up and back on your journey:

1. **Are you dwelling on the "should'ves" and "who-dunits"?** Okay, so it happened. You messed up. Don't sit around and blame everyone on the plane who was involved in your setback. You can't sit back and replay the failure over and over... it will just make you sick. Give yourself a little time to understand what happened. Sulk and cry if you need to, but get it out of your system. If you stay stuck in the past, you can't get to the future.

2. **Why did I get knocked down? Didn't I see it coming?** This is a hard one because it forces us to ask an honest question of ourselves. If we saw the challenge headed our way, then what does it say about us if we did not **get out of the way**? In my case, when I look at the times that I have failed (on Ric's deal, for instance), I knew I was headed for disaster. I knew I was taking on too much or stretched too far out of my comfort zone. I was just too stubborn to raise my hand for help. Be honest with yourself so that you can dodge the bullet the next time around.

3. **What did I learn?** As much as we hate to admit it, usually our setbacks represent the biggest opportunities for growth. It usually takes something dramatic for most of us to address the issues we knew were there all along. Use this as a time to improve. Like Einstein said, if you are doing the same thing over and over again and expecting different results, you just might be insane.

4. **What colored glasses do you choose?** We can control much of the outcomes of our lives by where we focus our energy and attention. We can choose to focus on the setbacks, or we can choose to focus on how to contribute to our success. Many people are afraid to focus on the positive things, to focus on their dreams because they

are afraid of failure. While that may seem safe, to me, its sounds like a slow walk toward an unfulfilling life. I would rather fail trying to achieve something great **instead of succeeding in doing nothing!**

The Story You Never Heard

There is a commonality when you read stories of successful individuals. Whether it's a great athlete, civic leader, or executive, there is always a story of accomplishment. We recount Steve Jobs' return to Apple with awe. We recount Bill Clinton's underdog presidential victory with inspiration. We celebrate their triumphant successes and often forget about the hurdles that they conquered to get there.

The story we never hear is the one about the man or woman who **never got back up** after being knocked down one too many times. We all know it happens. We all know of individuals who decided "enough is enough." We all know people who, when faced with the choice of getting up and fighting another round, decide to lay down and take the 10 count.

It doesn't necessarily mean that we are ashamed of those individuals; we just don't want to be them. There are times in life when we all have to take pause and regroup. But there is a difference between regrouping and giving up. You can trade one dream for another, but it's not okay to stop dreaming entirely. It's okay to decide to pursue a different path in life, but it's not okay to decide sit in the middle of the road until the end of days.

Well, at least, it's not okay for me. And if you're still reading this book, if you've come this far on the journey with me, then I doubt it's not "okay" for you, either.

I don't ask for perfection; only progress. All I ask is that you make your life a story that those who come after you will want to read... and keep your head out of the sand!

CHAPTER TWELVE

Encore

"So, here is the victory lap..."
~ Jay-Z, *Encore*

First and foremost, I want to say "thank you." Thank you for allowing me to spend time with you on your journey. But your journey is not over. Actually, you have a long road ahead of you. You have great things to do, lives to impact... an entire world to change, even if it's just your little corner of it. As Benjamin Mays once said, "We each have something distinctive to do in this world. If we don't do it, it will never get done."

If you remember one thing and one thing only, remember this:

It all comes down to being the **authentic individual** you. As we take our victory lap together, remember, I leave you with this:

- **Catch Your Wave:** *Timing is everything*

- **Don't Play Craps!:** *Take calculated risks*

- **It's Not the C.R.E.A.M.:** *Know what drives you*

- **What is Your Personal Brand?:** *Own your brand*

- **Swagger – Do You Have It in You?:** *Let your uniqueness shine*

- **King Kong Ain't Got Nothin' On Me:** *Be bold, be confident*

- **Can You Hustle?:** *You have to put the work in*

- **Make Your Own Path:** *Be a trailblazer*

- **Connecting Your Circle:** *Establish meaningful relationships*

- **No Substitute for Leadership:** *What more is there to say*

- **Get Back Up:** *We all fall down, but we remember those who get up*

Journey on, journey well... and hopefully, I will see you on the path. If our paths don't cross, please don't hesitate to visit me at www.rahardamon.com and drop me a line to let me know how you are doing. I'd love to hear about your progress, your ups and downs, how far you've come, and what it will take to get you the rest of the way!

Acknowledgements

No journey of any significance is ever taken alone. Mine is no different. My journey through life and the journey to write this book have been fascinating and complex, fun and traumatic, motivating and challenging.

To all who have been there along the way, I want to take this opportunity to say "thank you." I thank you for your interaction, challenges, support, counsel and sometimes just your mere presence. I even thank those who provided doubt and disbelief along the way, because you provided a different perspective from which I was able to view my journey.

To the Most High, thank you for the inspiration.

To my family, your constant support has been immeasurable. To my Mom, Dad, Kaili, RJ and Ella Monroe, brothers, sisters, cousins, aunts and uncles I say, with utmost sincerity and depth of gratitude, "Thank you, thank you."

To my friends and colleagues, thank you for the many experiences.

Last but not least – to each of you reading this, thank you for going on this journey with me. We can all get there (wherever your personal journey takes you), with a little help from our friends…

CPSIA information can be obtained at www.ICGtesting.com
Printed in the USA
BVOW080124210313

316055BV00002B/21/P